EXTORTION GAMES

REGULATING? OR CORPORATE BULLYING...?

For general information or to contact the author:
sylvia@slysolutions.ca
www.slysolutions.ca/contactme

ISBN
978-1-77370-528-6 (Hardcover)
978-1-77370-526-2 (Paperback)
978-1-77370-527-9 (eBook)

EXTORTION
GAMES

REGULATING? OR CORPORATE BULLYING...?

**A PURSUIT OF LIBERTY AGAINST A RELENTLESS,
MONOPOLIZING, AND TYRANNICAL REAL ESTATE COUNCIL**

SYLVIA LYNN GERMAIN

I dedicate this book to my beautiful daughter, Erin Jessica, who sadly had to witness the downfall of her Mother and bear the brunt of my stress during her very impressionable early teenage years. I appreciate all the love and support you gave, and still give me, and I hope that you will forgive me for leaning on you when you should have been leaning on me.

I hope this book will symbolize my renewing strength and a newfound pride in me as your Mother.

Love you to the moon and back, and back again

Love, Mom

xoxo

"I hope you never fear those mountains in the distance,
Never settle for the path of least resistance,
Living might mean taking chances but they're worth taking,
Loving might be a mistake but it's worth making.
Don't let some hell bent heart leave you bitter.
When you come close to selling out, reconsider.
Give the heavens above more than just a passing glance,
And when you get the choice to sit it out or dance,
I hope you dance..."

-Leanne Womack

Table of Contents

SECTION II – Bully Alert 59

SECTION III – In the Monopoly Ring 83

PART I – Fight #1

"

"Each time a man stands up for an ideal, or acts to improve the lot of others, or strikes out against injustice, he sends forth a tiny ripple of hope, and crossing each other from a million different centers of energy and daring those ripples build a current which can sweep down the mightiest walls of oppression and resistance."

Robert F. Kennedy

INTRODUCTION

I stare at the 2" pile of paper evidence I need to photocopy at least four times in preparation of a pre-trial conference in my counter suit defense against the Real Estate Council of Alberta (RECA). I wonder if it's worth my time and money or if I'm just being set up to be knocked back down by a Calgary Judge who is most likely in cahoots with the Real Estate Council of Alberta. The fact that this hearing is being held in Calgary where RECA has their offices versus in Edmonton or St. Albert, where I've done business for over 13 years, has me questioning if this Calgary judge is golf buddies with the executive director or solicitor for RECA. RECA should have had to file their claim in the Edmonton jurisdiction and it will cost me significantly more to request a transfer from their city to my city but I have no choice now but to pick myself up off the ground, dust myself off, and stand up and ROAR!

I cannot be the first innocent victim of this non-government regulatory organization, but I may be the first to fight back, and win. I am moved to stand up and shed some truthful light about the decline of ethics and integrity in government and regulatory council in this so called fairest land of all. I will most likely never get the *whole* story out in a pre-trial conference or in any court room and I feel that I have to publish my story with this book to somehow provide the means to an end.

I have been a believer that everything happens for a reason and that we all must hold ourselves accountable for our positions in life. I still stand strong though in that I NEVER did anything wrong, illegal, immoral, or unethical in my business practice. I do understand and appreciate the importance of rules to protect the public. I agree that there is a very fine line between my landlord business activities and real estate property manager activities but that line is there. That line is drawn between the Residential Tenancies Act and the Real Estate Act. I deserve to have that line recognized. My clients deserve it as well.

I understand the hierarchy in the corporate world and that most people feel safe and comfortable being part of a pecking order and having limited responsibility. I am not most people. I am an independent business woman who thrives in the involvement with the entire operation, not just a piece of it. We all have a natural right to shine brighter than others without being forced to dim our own light.

My cooperation in answering RECA's initial interrogative questions was never recognized, reinforcing the belief that the Real Estate Council of Alberta never did have reason to take me down other than jealousy, greed and a hunger for power. I am confident that most of you reading this book, to the end, will come to the same conclusion. I was deemed guilty before even being questioned and it was RECA's mission to prove me guilty with no regard for my real position. I simply disrupted their dictatorial and authoritative industry with a competitive and advanced business model that presented transparency.

This is a factual story and I have chosen to name most real names, not fictional names. My reputation was not respected on the World Wide Web so I do not see the need in protecting any of their identities. Fictional names mask the truth and I am sharing the truth. I have, however, protected names of clients and tenants and those who requested to be anonymous. This book includes every email and letter correspondence between myself and RECA. It also includes the pivotal email correspondence from the instigator of this extortion. All inserts are in chronological order as the story unfolds.

Bullying has been a highly recognized and publicized concern regarding the nation's youth in our schools and playgrounds and seems to be escalating with the rapid advances in technology. Our youth learn bullying behaviour from the adult examples they are subject to. Adult bullying can be even more detrimental and life altering than childhood bullying, as you will learn in my story, and it needs to be recognized and addressed. Maybe if we set better examples in the adult world, we will be able to better influence our youth.

SECTION 1

About the Author

PART I

The Yellow Brick Road to Becoming an Entrepreneur

CHAPTER 1
In the Beginning

The life path that has led me here is relevant to understanding why I endured all the stresses and insanity of remaining a Landlord Agent as long as I have, and why I endured the past years of harassment and defamation of my personal and business character by the Real Estate Council of Alberta.

It was never my dream to be a Landlord Agent. Go figure. I was only 17 when I moved away on my own from the small Northern town in Alberta where I was raised. My father's income came from fur trapping and trading plus seasonal construction and labour jobs, and my mother's income from government administration positions and other part time businesses. The family line was built around farming versus white collar positions that required higher levels of education and there wasn't a surplus of money to be considering cushiony college funds. I did graduate high school with an advanced matriculation diploma, similar to the modern honours scale, but college or university wasn't in the stars for me. Nevertheless, I did learn the value of money and budgeting at a young age from the small allowances I would receive and the money my father would raise for me with deposit refunds from all the bottles he would collect on the side of the road. Dad would stop on the side of the highway every time he spotted a bottle in the ditch. This kept my little savings account growing as a child and by the time I was 6 years old I was buying my very own flowered banana seat bicycle with tassels on the handle bars. I still remember the smell of the vinyl wrapped seat and I have never felt more empowered in my life. I loved that empowered feeling and I knew then that I would always do what I had to do to get what I wanted.

My parents taught me the value of honesty, integrity, and hard work. Both my parents always did what they had to do. Dad would give the shirt off his back to help anyone. He said what he meant and always meant what he said. Mom also worked hard juggling different businesses on top of working in the garden that took up most of the second lot that made up our property. In the winter Dad would turn that garden plot into a huge skating rink for me and my younger brother. I come from a long line of good people with strong home-grown ethics both in business and with family and friends.

I was bullied in school though. The mean girls were disenchanted with the DD breast cups that I was naturally blessed with at the young age of 12. (I believe it's been more a curse than a blessing) Being a bit of a tomboy, who loved fishing with my dad and building forts with the neighbourhood boys and smokin' in the boys' room did not present favourably to the mean girls either. I spent grades 9 through 12 avoiding the girls' washrooms during breaks to save myself from being accosted. This is what school principals suggested as the only way to avoid confrontation. "Don't go where they are" is what I was told. I would also always have to wait for 30 minutes after school, after all the buses were gone, before walking home. I had been caught off guard being ambushed by tribes of aboriginal girls enough times that it was just worth the extra wait. I would sometimes hangout at the propane station at the corner across from the school and visit with Rob until I thought the coast was clear. It got so bad at one point in Grade 11 that I began carrying a 4" blade with me just for an added sense of security. I never dreamed of ever using it though. The violence in that high school got so bad that the Edmonton Journal interviewed me for a story they published in 1985. I did actually pull that knife out of my back pocket one day but that's part of another book that's in me to write. Suffice it to say I was learning hard lessons.

I fell in love with the bad boy in high school and although I fraternized in many different social circles I was always being warned by teachers and councillors to stay away from the bad boys or I would not amount to anything. The bad boys were not bad people. They were just more street smart than book smart. They were boys looking to belong to something. How dare teachers imprint such negative energy upon young impressionable minds? I could amount to whatever I wanted to amount to no matter who I befriended. *I'll show them,* I thought with conviction.

Although I graduated with an advanced matriculation diploma at 17 years, I had absolutely no plan. All I knew was that I wanted to spread my wings and learn the meaning of life by travelling and building a life of my own in a city I could escape and hide in. I wanted the freedom to become whatever I would choose to be.

Strong values, survival skills and empty pockets are all I was packing with me when I decided to move to the big city lights of Edmonton, Alberta. I had seen much bigger cities with many more lights over the years but at that time, at 17 years old, it was the closest land of opportunity for me. It was 1987, I had gotten my first job in the retail industry with Mariposa, a women's fashion store, and knew a friend of a friend who was going to let me cop a squat in her apartment until I got established on my own two feet.

I was so bored with the retail job of standing around all day just waiting for that odd customer who actually wanted help with finding a different size. I had only been there two months and feeling like I was not making a difference in my life, or anyone else's life. The blisters on my heels from my new shoes were killing me and as I had been organizing and hanging clothes from a new shipment, I imagined myself squatting in that pile of clothes just to take a load off for a minute. There wasn't anyone in the store so "What could it hurt?" I thought. Well, I learned I would get fired. That hurt my ego and I had to find another job right away because I had rent to pay.

The Brick Warehouse, a home furnishing retail store, was hiring sales associates and offering the kind of money and commissions I wanted. I went in to that downtown head office dressed with my skirt, blazer, and high heels on (with band aids on my heels) not fazed by the fact I had just been fired from an even lower ranked retail position. I held my head high believing I looked the part for that sales associate position. The guy interviewing me was a little concerned about my lack of experience in sales but he seemed to get a kick out of my determined attitude and offered me a job in their finance department analyzing credit applications. Perfect.

Christmas came and went and so did staff at The Brick Warehouse due to declining sales. Those short five months in that finance department did however pave the yellow brick road for me into the financial industry. I spent almost two years with NearBank Financial Centres managing store operations by myself in different locations throughout Edmonton. It was a cheque cashing business for those who did not qualify for higher luxury bank accounts and it was my job to do the necessary background checks to limit the risk of bouncing cheques. I had many other responsibilities of course, including photo taking and cleaning of the store. The day I realized that one of the neighbourhood drunks had passed out in my camera booth room and peed all over it, I decided it was time for me to move up town with a real bank that did not have plexi-glass securing me from the customers or 12 hour days.

I became that uptown girl with Royal Trust on Jasper Avenue in downtown Edmonton. This is when banker's hours really were still banker's hours, 10:00 am – 2:00 pm. Sweet. Every rose has its thorn though and those hours were full out with no time to pee. I must have set a bar though because they offered me extra hours with the option to open at 9:00 am as the single teller. Always up for a challenge, I took it. I did not realize how busy that first hour would be with line ups out the door and the phone ringing off the hook that I needed to be back up to answer. Holy #$%^!! I'm not sure how I managed to excel in upselling other banking services while I was multi-tasking so busily but I'm proud to brag that I was one of ten Royal Trust staff in Alberta to receive the Royal Circle Award for sales.

That pace was hard to maintain though and I felt like I was selling just to sell. The threat of robbery was always very high in the downtown city core as well and the mandatory monthly robbery procedure training scared me into looking for something a little safer and slower paced.

Firefighters Credit Union was an excellent fit for me. Service based on strong ethics and values plus profit sharing with members. At 19 years old that made sense to me. Fire Fighters Credit Union merged with Police Credit Union to become Emergency Services Credit Union and that merger presented advancement opportunities for me. For 13 years, within that Credit Union, I worked and educated my way up from p/t bank teller to f/t teller to investment officer, Mutual Fund Advisor, marketing assistant, accounting and audit assistant, consumer lender, mortgage lender, and was on my way to completing the financial planner component. I was always taking evening courses at NAIT in Business Administration and other required business courses through the Credit Union Institute of Canada. I was a go-getter.

In 1996 I married Chris, who I had met through a dating agency. We built a new custom home in the suburb of St. Albert and on May 25, 2000 I became a mother to the most beautiful strawberry blonde, blue eyed blessing that is my daughter.

Becoming a mother is life changing for all but I could have never been prepared for what would happen when I chose to go back to work and put my daughter in the hands of someone I did not know.

> *"Everyone has experienced something that has changed them in a way that they could never go back to the person they once were."*
> **- Anonymous**

CHAPTER 2
A Defining Moment

I loved my job in banking and took it very seriously. So seriously that I was calling the other personal banker in the middle of birth contractions at the hospital to go over all my client files so service to my clients wouldn't be disrupted. I was 30 years old and still full of energy and I had every intention of being a great mother with an office job. I did go back to my banking role after an extended maternity leave not expecting that the universe would have a much different plan for me. I will never forget that day.

Eight months after being back at work, I sat in my comfy burgundy velvet office chair fit for a queen at my big mahogany desk covered in an organized mess of mortgage and loan client files. I stared out the windows that surrounded me and thought, "Why am I here?" I should be with my little girl. Of course there was typical red tape that led up to me thinking these thoughts and over the 10 years there I had often wished I could tell the boss to shove it, but this moment was different. So different that I called up my husband and told him I was going to quit my job and hand in my resignation that day.

He couldn't believe what he was hearing and concerned about not discussing the financial hit of a decision like that. However, knowing me, he knew I must have good reason so he supported me in the best way he could have by suggesting that I take a walk to calm myself and if after one hour I was still feeling this strongly, then he would support my decision to quit my job.

This calming process required some deep breathing on my part so I bummed a cigarette from one of the girls in the office, despite the fact that I wasn't a regular smoker, and set out on my mission. I found a park bench to sit on and smoke my cigarette, and I sat there inhaling that cigarette smoke as deeply as I could asking the question in my mind 'What am I supposed to do with my life?' Like most of us, I have pondered this question thousands of times I'm sure but this time was different. This time I heard an answer. Just as though an angel were sitting right beside me I heard, very clearly and distinctively, "Sylvia, you do not need this job anymore. You NEED to be at home to raise your daughter". It wasn't just a thought. I heard it with my ears and it resonated in me so strongly with body tingles that I immediately walked back to my office and wrote up my resignation and handed it in.

I've had more than a few defining moments in my life and this has been the biggest so far and soon you will understand why.

I had been at home for only two weeks after my final day at the Credit Union. I was eating dinner with my husband and our daughter while watching the 6 o'clock news when a story came on about a day home provider in St. Albert, Alberta who was under investigation for allegedly drugging up to 26 children that had been in her care on a daily basis. They found 11 baby exersaucers in a hidden room in her basement and numerous cribs. I was horrified by this story and already feeling grateful for not needing to have my daughter in a day home anymore. I do not even know how to describe what I felt a few short moments later when the TV camera crew zoomed in on the home of this heartless monster of a woman, and it was the very day home I had been bringing my daughter to 5 days per week for 8 months.

I swear my heart fell right out of my chest onto the coffee table and the blood drained from my whole body while hundreds of images flashed through my mind remembering all the moments that my intuition had been tugging at me that something just wasn't right with that day home or that woman.

The red flags were explained away; I had thought I was just being paranoid. Why was the house always so neat and tidy? Why were the toys never out of place? When did this woman find the time and energy to paint her living room walls a different colour? Because she is a high energy perfectionist go-getter, I explained. Why did I never hear screaming kids running around when I picked up my daughter or dropped her off? Because this woman had them well trained, I explained. Why was my daughter always so sleepy when I picked her up at 5:00 pm? Because she was too energized by day home activity through the day, this woman explained. Why did my daughter always have a diaper rash during the week that cleared up on the weekend when I cared for her? Because I used better quality non-toxic ointments, I explained, and she obviously wasn't using what I gave her. Why were my daughter's eyes so red underneath? Because she's a fair skinned red head I explained. Why would it take so long for this woman to answer the door when I did surprise visits? Because she's the kind of woman who wanted to tidy everything up first, I explained. I was literally sick to my stomach with this slap-in-the-face realization.

The answer to all these red flags was that my daughter was being drugged with codeine and left to sit in an exersaucer to sleep in a wet diaper all day, while this criminally unstable woman enjoyed her days redecorating and raking in the cash from naïve first-time mother's like me.

How could I have been so ignorant of what was going on?! How could I have not taken my daughter's diaper rash and red eyes more seriously? How could I have disregarded the question of why those toys and books looked like they were never used? How could I have believed that children under 5 could be so well trained and not be running around? How could I ever forgive myself for letting this happen to my daughter? How?!

I initially doubted my gut instincts because I told myself I had followed all the steps I was taught when looking for child care. I had gone to community support programs to have access to all the resources for new moms and to establish relationships with other new moms. I had weighed the pros and cons of day care versus day home. I had visited day cares and 5 other day homes advertising at that time. The other day homes I visited were filthy with providers who smoked or had too many pets. When I came across Lorna's day home it was so perfect.

The basement was set up like a colourful day care with the perfect books, toys, tables, and chairs, and relaxing areas to suit any and every child. There were swings and toys in the back yard that was immaculate. The whole house was spotless. Lorna claimed to have the best credentials with educational background in psychology and sociology and had been previously employed by Alberta Hospital and had references to back that up. She laid out a wonderful healthy snack and eating plan that hooked me. She made sure to schedule our initial visit on a Sunday when she wouldn't be distracted by the job and be able to give me her full attention, which was a big mistake on my part.

I had come home from that meeting telling my husband that this day home was perfect but that it just seemed too perfect, like one of those too good to be true kind of perfects. He suggested I trust my gut on that and keep looking but I was expected back at work in one week and running out of time. I called the references she gave me and one was a neighbour who was presently using her. This turned into the same neighbour who was home from work sick one day and noticed the alarming number of vehicles and parents dropping off their children at Lorna's that day. It was significantly more than the government regulated limit of 6 and this neighbour set up her own video camera the next day that recorded 25 children being dropped off that day, and is what instigated the investigation. I also knew of one of the girls I met in the mom and baby community group that had also just hired Lorna. This new mom and her husband were both lawyers and had supposedly done some background checks on Lorna as well, and I thought if anyone would have completed a thorough back ground check to rely on it would be a lawyer.

The next year included a coming together of all the parents affected by this conniving woman and providing hair samples from our children to prove the traces of codeine from the Tylenol she was administering to them and trying to secure legal counsel for a larger lawsuit vs individual lawsuits. The limited and unguaranteed gain wasn't worth the cost to many and the group fell apart. News coverage eventually reported that she was fined $3000. That's all. The physical threat and damage that this woman imposed upon our 26 children and the mental anguish suffered by me and her father and the other 50 parents was believed to be worth much more than $3000. She was able to just sell her home and do it all over again in a new place in B.C. while some of us were left scarred for life and some marriages were strained from the guilt, including mine, that lead to my divorce.

The question of how many other day home providers were doing the same thing always burned in my mind like a hot branding iron and I vowed that I would never leave my daughter unprotected or in the care of a stranger ever again. The corporate 9 to 5 job was not in my cards anymore because I didn't have the family or friend resources to help with before school or after school care even when she was old enough to start school. I could never find a job that paid enough to make before or after school care worth it. That is when I realized I would have to be self-employed with some kind of business from home, but what kind of business…?

CHAPTER 3
Finding the Right Fit

After searching through the small lists of on-line courses available I decided on Personal Fitness Training as I was always a pro-active person with my own health. I completed correspondence courses though NAIT and Can-Fit-Pro and got certified as a Personal Fitness Trainer. Working for a gym did not pay enough to keep me afloat so, I tried to be creative with a unique self-employed approach. I put together a program for the new Moms and Babies community support group in St. Albert and was lucky to get the space for free and charge $10 per mom. It was a 30 minute cardio/weight bearing routine for moms and babies utilizing babies for the weight and consisted of functional fitness moves that tied into nursery rhyme songs. We did plie squats to Old MacDonald Had a Farm, bridges to London Bridge, sit ups to One, Two, Buckle My Shoe, and overhead presses to Row, Row, Row Your Boat. You get the idea?

It was so much fun and the best thing of all was that I could bring my daughter with me as my own baby weight. The worst thing was that even with classes of 10-15 moms 2 times per week, it would never make me enough money to afford to keep raising my daughter in our home. I was also embarking on an unfortunate divorce journey and wasn't going to receive spousal support for longer than one year maximum so I needed to find something else. Fast.

I tried supplementing my income with business endeavours like Melaleuca and was initially successful with that but I did not care for the cold calling and high levels of constant networking that is required to remain successful in multi-level marketing business. I felt like I was being fake with people all the time and that they were being fake with me. I never benefited from networking luncheons; I only ended up with others always just chasing me to support their business. I needed something much more reliable. Even faster now.

Many people in my circle suggested I consider real estate but every time I spoke with a real estate broker about what this entailed, I couldn't help leaving each meeting thinking that it would probably cost me more money to maintain being a realtor than I would make. At that time online courses were not as popular and I did not have the child care options to assist me with being able to be in the classroom during the required hours. It would take more than $2500 to pay for the courses and then typically $500/month to pay fees to some broker just for an office and a marketing umbrella. There were other annual fees and constant educating and more fees. It didn't make sense to me. If I was going to be entrepreneurial I wanted to make money for me, not for someone else. The market has always been oversaturated with realtors and I would have had to spend all my weekends in open houses and wouldn't be able to bring my daughter to sit with me for that. Besides, I did not have the money for the courses.

I had to buy my ex-husband out on our home and owed him $60,000 based on the increased value. $30,000 came from RRSP's and $30,000 was added to the mortgage I took over. I was lucky that my Credit Union looked at my strong character and blemish free credit rating and allowed this mortgage transfer in my name even though I did not have full time income. Money was certainly tight and I lived hand to mouth for quite some time and relied on rental income from renting out the 3rd bedroom in my house to women who were also in divorce transition.

In my early 20's I was accustomed to posting rental ads in my apartment building and at colleges and universities for roommates. I had over 10 different roommates over the years and had always done a great job in picking them out so I wasn't scared to do the same thing even though I had a daughter to protect as well. When I was 24 I had completed a business course at the U of A thinking I would start up a Roommate finding service seeing as I had practical experience with that. I was going to name it Three's Company Roommate Finders. I actually still have the documents from the Nuans name search I did for it in 1994. I never did follow through with it because it was not a service that would make any amount of money. When I stopped to think about it more, how much could someone who needed a roommate to pay the bills be able to afford to pay me for the service…? Not enough.

My mother was actually a housing manager with the Government of Alberta for many years and it never once occurred to me to follow her footsteps. The idea just fell into my lap. I'm still not sure if I was really meant to be a landlord agent. When I think back to all the challenges I have faced with it and continue to face I know it is definitely not a dream business but it has remunerated well and allowed me to be a present mother.

It was back in 2003 when, Gerry, a guy I knew from the Personal Best self-improvement courses I completed in 2002 approached me about helping him out with finding new tenants for a four-plex he owned in Edmonton. He had moved to Calgary and he remembered that I had a background in consumer and mortgage lending with marketing experience, not to mention my experience in screening roommates for myself, and he thought I would be perfect for showing the unit, helping him screen renters, and completing the paperwork.

This seemed to be a step up from my roommate finding service idea. I needed any cash I could get my hands on and it was something I could pack my daughter along with me for so I agreed. I forget what he paid me for that but I remember it wasn't very much. He was satisfied enough with the tenants I signed in though that he called on me for the next tenant replacement he needed in that four-plex.

Initially he was posting and paying for the rental ads himself with his phone number and would transfer them to me to arrange a time for showings. We both found this to be extremely cumbersome and when I suggested that he post my contact number in the ads, he saw the value in streamlining that process and it wasn't long before he was asking me to write up the ads myself for higher pay.

Gerry had seen the potential in me to build something from this service I was providing to him, and his circle of family and business associates, and offered to have me stand in for him at a weekend seminar in Edmonton.

That Quick Start Program presented by Don R. Campbell of the Real Estate Investment Network (REIN) was phenomenal. Many of you reading this right know are familiar with this name and probably read Don R. Campbell's books *Real Estate Investing in Canada*, *Secrets of the Canadian Real Estate Cycle* and *Buying U.S. Real Estate* just to name a few. If you have not, you should. Don R. Campbell is a renowned real estate market analyzer and has been seen and heard on numerous radio and TV networks including BNN.

I had no idea what to expect from these 2 1/2 full days, but I was, and still am, very grateful to Gerry for granting me that opportunity. I was not ready to become an investor but based on what I saw at that program that weekend, I knew I could carve a niche for myself working for those investors. The resources, tools, and tricks I gathered from this seminar are what I still use 13 years later, plus a few more I've implemented through experience of course, to attract, secure, and manage 5 star tenants. I kick myself every time I get a little lazy and stray from these tried and true tricks because they work.

Gerry had a business partner in Calgary, who owned other properties, who also called on me a few times and he had family members with investment properties as well who called on me. There was a realtor in their circle as well who started referring investors to me every month, and then those investors started referring other investors to me for tenant placement services. I was able to increase my fees without any uproar and realized I was actually paying the bills with only 2 new clients every month.

The demand for cleaning services came part and parcel as well. Tenants who were moving out were less likely to care about how clean they left the property. They really cared how clean it was when moving in though. It was much less hassle to sign in new tenants without having to mark "still needs cleaning" on every line of the condition report, and having them state that they shouldn't have to leave it clean when they left if it was not clean for them moving in. So, I would arrive at the property prepared with my cleaning products when I did a sign out walk through with a tenant and put in an extra few well paid hours of cleaning and minor repairs before the next tenant came in. The client would pay me from that move out tenant's security deposit.

These cleaning services provided money I really needed to earn but there was not always much time in between signing one tenant out and signing the next one in. It became necessary to streamline this inspection process when I became busier with more than three tenant move outs on the last day of every month. This is when I implemented an even more detailed cleaning list for the moving out tenants to follow in order to ensure a full refund of their security deposit. Being up front with the tenants about what was expected, and the amount that they would be charged for incomplete cleaning, motivated them to do their best. It also protected me from them stomping their feet about any unfair charges on their security deposit refund statements. Funny thing though how the same things are still missed by almost everyone such as bathroom fans, baseboards, moving the fridge and stove, doors, switches, ceiling fans, and blinds. I still always have my cleaning bucket ready for these forgotten items.

It wasn't an easy job or glorifying by any stretch, and there were times I almost puked. I was sometimes appalled at the kind of tenants some of my clients had trusted with their investment properties. I've cleaned more than one property that had layers of urine around the base of the toilet, both human and dog urine and feces on walls and ceilings, and rotting food in cupboards and fridges with mould growing in and behind fridges and ovens. *Gag.* I am such a squeaky clean person and if I wasn't thick skinned before getting into this line of work, I would soon be.

CHAPTER 4
The One Stop Shop

I quickly realized how valuable my service was and that clients would be willing to pay top dollar to avoid all this yuck by having the right tenants.

My circle of friends and family had been asking for a few years already why I wasn't building this landlord agent business of mine into the Trump Empire it could be, haha. Kidding. Seriously though, there was obviously a demand for tenant placement services that the property management industry wasn't offering because for 5 years I was earning a living from just these tenant placement services and referrals.

I was still packing my daughter along with me when I had to during day time showings and cleaning. She was my right hand girl and I would set her on the floor on a blanket with a book and snacks if I was cleaning. She was actually my lucky charm during showings and I believe that it was because potential tenants could relate to me as more friendly and approachable. More real.

Clients were appreciating how simple it was to deal with me and how much time and hassle they saved in not having to coordinate cleaners. My extended services quickly led to small touch up repairs and painting. I was exercising my creative design talents with cost-effective and tasteful suggestions for property improvements that would attract the right tenant, for the right price, and the right time but also improve resale value. Clients always loved my suggestion to use white faux wood blinds versus cheaper aluminum ones as they were much longer lasting, easier to clean, and more resilient. They loved my ability to choose practical flooring options and lighting packages and some clients even allowed me to experiment with bold feature wall paint colours to stand out from the crowd and secure great tenants quicker.

A one stop shop is what I had become. Consumers love one stop shopping. It's one of the reasons Walmart is so successful. Back in my Credit Union banking days we structured our staff to be able to handle almost any transaction so that clients would not have to be turned away when they came in for service. Customers did not like being told that the "specialist" was not available. We were full service staff with front line tellers opening and closing accounts, posting RRSP/GIC transactions, wire transfers, upselling credit cards, etc. In these modern days I have to schedule an appointment to open a simple savings account and nobody has an answer for anything anymore without having to ask somebody else who is the specialist in that area. Administrative hierarchy has become a priority over customer service in this millennial age and I think it really is a service shame.

My real estate investor clients appreciated getting one stop shopping full service or just a la carte service as much as my banking clients had appreciated the one stop in my office. My previous banking clients could open a chequing account, a savings account with an auto transfer set up, order cheques, deposit cash, get a debit card and a credit card, get pre-approved for a car loan or mortgage, and get investment advice all in one appointment with me. Full service is just how I was trained to roll and it rolls smoother that way.

My real estate clients were spoiled by the cost effectiveness and time savings in having me perform all landlord duties. They knew if they could trust me with the ad placements, paperwork, cleaning, improvements, and placing the right tenants, they could trust me to handle everything.

Clients were now wanting to hire me to handle the 24/7 managing of their tenants and maintenance of their properties seeing how familiar I was with their property already. Hmmm...I would have to think about that.

I was apprehensive about taking on the 24/7 landlord role. It was one thing to do some prep work, screening, and paperwork and pass the ongoing maintenance back to the owner, but did I really want to have tenants calling me in the middle of the night or on Sundays about their problems? I just was not ready for that. I thought I should probably test owning my own rental property first.

Having at least one of my own rental properties would round out my knowledge to be able to relate to my investor clients that much better. Besides, I was already 38 years old without a pension plan, and needed to start building some kind of retirement plan funding besides the mutual funds and other high risk investments that weren't getting me anywhere. I had equity built up in my house but not enough to afford a property in the Edmonton area so I went to Phoenix.

It was 2008 and Phoneix, Arizona was experiencing the start of a buyer's market with significant drops in property values and foreclosures and 'short sales' were cropping up everywhere. I took out my REIN Quick Start Bible to refresh what I learned about scoring a property and spent 6 months researching on line for the perfect investment opportunities in Phoenix.

I found 1 bedroom resort complex units for $75,000 US that were valued at $220,000 US the previous year. Condo fees were only $140 US/month and property taxes were $650 US/year. Even with the Canadian currency exchange I had a cash flow property even at the lowest rent amount of $700 US/month.

One flight to Phoenix to view the unit and I had a signed deal in my hand. I thought paying cash would make the process simpler but even with cash, the paperwork took 5 months to close everything. It was so time consuming and I couldn't imagine going through it again, especially if I required a mortgage. I dislike red tape, and the U.S.A is all about the red tape.

I lucked out in finding Real Property Management in Phoenix who also provided me with a great tenant placement service, allowing me to manage the tenant after they signed him in. It's been 8 years (at the time I write this) and this tenant is still renting there. I was very pleased with that tenant finding service at Real Property Management. It was comparable to my own services.

I've had 2 repairs in all these 8 years. A screen door and replacement of the air conditioning. Both of these issues were dealt with easily with one phone call to excellent service providers in Phoenix who took the stress off me with a seamless process. The air conditioner unit was replaced and invoiced within 48 hours. I cannot even get anyone to quote anything for me here in Alberta within 48 hours. I have to surprisingly admit that managing my own US condo investment property has been easier and less hectic than many of the hassles I've experienced here in Alberta with tenants and some service providers.

I was determined to have some more of this rental residual income but I couldn't afford property in my area at their high market values and there was way too much red tape and tax implications to consider another US purchase.

Managing other clients' properties and not having to buy the investment properties myself made complete sense to me at the time. I would always have the positive cash flow without the money up front, or expenses associated with repairs and improvements.

I had already been doing a great job independently maintaining and renovating my own executive home on a corner lot in St. Albert, and had a few homes I was already managing for a few select clients so I started thinking, how hard could it really be to be on call 24/7 for 20 more properties...? Well, the answer to that is in another upcoming book...

PART II

A Corporation is Born

CHAPTER 5
Build it and They Will Come

So I had been successfully placing tenants for 6 years at this point but still renting out my 3rd bedroom and taking on short term accounting and charity work positions here and there and dating the wrong men to make ends meet. I was ready to take this landlord service to the next level of 24/7 management so I did not have to rely on roommates and boyfriends anymore.

I was cut out to be an independent business woman. I enrolled in an 8 week long government sponsored small business government program through Anderson Career Training Institute (ACTI). I was going to get a real business plan together and do this right. In the couple months I was waiting for the course to commence I focused heavily on my marketing skills, formatting basic website information on power point and researching logos. My business model was the competitive edge that I needed to showcase in my website advertising. One edge was the fact that I provided a la carte tenant placement services for residential owners with a very high success rate already of finding the right tenants very quickly. The real estate industry was not providing this service. They were only providing property management services that entailed the controlling of all security deposit and rent money on long term contracts. Their business model was more geared to commercial management of entire apartment buildings, not one individually owned condo unit.

The other edge I had was that I also provided ongoing tenant and property management services but did not control security deposits or rent money. It was very transparent that way. If I did not hold their money I could not mismanage it and there was nothing to regulate. The owners paid me to do all the work involved in placing and managing tenants for them. I coordinated property repairs and the owners paid the bills directly to the repair company. It was simple and a win-win for all and had been working very smoothly for 6 years already. The referrals coming in proved the public wanted it.

The ACTI course itself was very instrumental in drawing up a professional business plan and client contracts. My tenant placement client contracts were one page in length. My property management contracts were 3 pages in length. Both contracts clearly laid out my responsibilities as a landlord agent and the responsibilities of the owner, as well as the cost and payment structure. They also included a 60 day satisfaction guarantee on new tenants. I was so confident that I could find the right tenant, for the right price, for the right time that I offered to replace any dud tenant needing eviction in the first 60 days at no extra cost. NOBODY did this. These client contracts were collaborated on with legal counsel in great detail as part of the ACTI program.

The Residential Tenancies Act allowed for laxity in who a residential owner could designate as their agent so the only license I was expected to have was a business license to operate.

Incorporating my business name was greatly encouraged in order to protect my personal reputation and assets should unfortunate circumstances challenge me legally. At that time I could not imagine how unfortunate some circumstances could really be. In hindsight, in my experience with RECA, I can say that incorporating does not protect your personal name.

I actually came up with my business name while I was sitting in a hot tub with a glass of wine, at a girlfriend's home in Red Deer. All my life people have spelled my name incorrectly as Slyvia versus Sylvia. The writing hand seems to find Sly easier to write out than Syl so, the nickname Sly came about. I was also known to be a very creative and resourceful gal who had designed a very sly business model. The words Sly Solutions Ltd just rolled out sending me a chill up my spine in the bubbling hot water. I've had some feedback from people here and there with raised eyebrows thinking the term "Sly" comes across as crooked or conniving but my transparency made me trustworthy enough for the majority of clients to actually appreciate my nick name. I kept the tagline *Right Tenants, Right Price, Right Time.*

The ongoing support from instructors in this ACTI program was very valuable. I was disappointed to learn that the Alberta Government had discontinued this program for a few years but happy to find out that it has since been reinstated. You can find contact information in my Resource section. I highly recommend it for those who are committed to being an entrepreneur. This program provided me with all the tools I needed to fly high. I made some great friends and contacts in this course that were also a key factor in growing my network of tradespeople.

The referrals for website building and hosting, at the time, were not as impressive. Website developers I spoke to had wanted thousands of dollars and could not even provide me any bonus features or anything that wowed me. I needed to be able to make changes myself easily and did not understand their website platforms. One of my classmates referred me to www.vistaprint.ca and I was thoroughly impressed with this company.

www.vistaprint.ca offered hundreds of website templates to choose from with matching business cards, letterhead, banners, vehicle magnets, pens, caps, email registering, statistic reports, SEO optimization…everything I needed to market and track my business professionally and cost effectively. I did not require a separate host and it was free for me to customize a very functional 5 page website that cost less than $25/month to maintain. It was perfect for a do-it-yourself girl like me. Their support service was second to none. I was always assisted by the first representative I spoke to versus being transferred endlessly to the wrong department like many other companies. I already had my basic text set out in PowerPoint and just cut and pasted to Vistaprint and, voila! I had an impressive website.

On February 23, 2009, Sly Solutions Ltd was registered as a corporation with a website (www.slysolutions.ca), business cards, business license, and a business plan with a committed goal of purchasing a 4x4 truck within three months and reaching $60,000 in revenue by the end of that year.

I had also paid for a membership with the Edmonton Apartment Association (EAA) They are now called Alberta Residential Landlord Association (ARLA) to have access to professional forms and notices and updates on landlord and tenancy laws. Once I had my business license and EAA/ARLA membership I was able to get an account with Tenant

Verification Services to be able to have access to tenant credit check information. I was set and l took off like a rocket ship into space.

I used Kijiji to test my 1st attempt in advertising my service and website. Within one week of placing that little ad I had a signed contract in place with a new investor client who transferred 13 of her condo units to me to manage for one year, while she embarked on a once in a life time motorcycle journey with her husband in South America. I was SO jealous!! That's still on my bucket list to do. I need the boyfriend first though because I've already proven I make a better motorcycle passenger then operator! I owned my own motorcycle for 3 weeks before selling it. But back to my business story…

I could hardly believe this gal trusted me from a Kijiji ad and one meeting but she did know that if I was practicing Don Campbell's REIN (Real Estate Investment Network) processes than her properties would be in good hands. She was a member of REIN and some of the forms and checklists I still use today come from her. I'm so grateful to her for that one year long opportunity. I learned so much from the experience, mostly what properties NOT to take on again, haha, but more about eviction processes.

I thought if I could get business like that from a small Kijiji ad I was bound to get great clients from actual rental websites that allowed property managers/landlord agents to advertise a small blurb. I owe a great deal of gratitude to Cindy from www.rentedmonton.com who was intrigued by my a la carte business model. Cindy was the gal who came up with the term "Custom Property Management" that has differentiated my services from licensed real estate industry professionals. She claimed that many people would call them looking for referrals for just tenant placement services or sign-in and sign-out inspections and she had nobody to refer these people to. I was the first one trying to offer and advertise this service. It was Cindy at www.rentedmonton.com that gave me the credible boost I needed by allowing me to advertise on their reputable site. Thank you Cindy!

By June 2009, three months after incorporating, I had already signed enough clients to get that truck I put down as a goal in my business plan. I paid cash for a 2008 White Dodge Dakota 4x4 V8 and slapped some Sly Solutions Ltd marketing vehicle magnets on the side doors and back bumper sticker that matched my website and business cards. The large door magnets cost less than $20. I was geared up now for hauling materials for minor property renovations.

I found myself gathering girlfriends and boyfriends to help me tear out carpets and lay laminate, tear out kitchens and replace cabinets and plumbing. I learned to replace lighting fixtures myself, and was measuring and cutting new baseboards and trim, tearing out and laying flooring, removing wallpaper, and playing with faux paint finishes. I was having fun now and making money. By the end of that year in 2009 I had surpassed my $60,000 revenue goal. My business and my life was on a roll. I was reaping the rewards for my hard work.

The Better Business Bureau even reached out to me to get accreditation with them as they also would get inquiries for referrals to trustworthy property managers. Please note, I did not approach BBB. They approached me. I knew I had a satisfaction guaranteed service that would earn me an A+ rating. It made sense to pay for the added boost for stronger credibility. The added BBB logo on my website did earn me that extra credibility. Clients were approaching me with rare executive homes that fetched $2000-$4000/ month in rent. Some were contracting me from all ends of the world. I even had clients as far as the Bahamas and Australia. Some of these clients were referred but most clients chose me over others they found advertised on www.rentedmonton.com and www.rentfaster.ca based on my transparent business model, even though my fees were higher and they had never met me. Think about that for a minute.

Sometimes it astounded me that people would trust me so easily after one email and one telephone correspondence but I guess it was simple. They had less to lose with my service based on my transparent business model and contract, and I proved myself as professional and trustworthy. I walked my talk.

I had built a successful and lucrative business with less than $1000 start up. With success comes challenges though.

CHAPTER 6
Growing Pains

Sometimes I was working 10-14 hour days with all the driving to all ends of Edmonton from my home office in St. Albert. One hundred condo units would be easy to manage all in one apartment complex, but I had condo units and duplexes and executive homes spread throughout all corners of Edmonton and St. Albert and one in Fort Saskatchewan. At month end I would sometimes have 5 sign-outs and 5 sign-ins all in one day at different ends of the city. Eating wasn't even an option on days like that and I actually lost weight that year. Woohoo! The paperwork to get distributed to clients and banking deposits took another few days and I still had to be on call handling everything that could and would come up with managing tenants and properties and trust me, that list is endless. No matter how tedious it became I never ignored a call or text or email.

I was disbelievingly turning away business every single day. People were calling me from surrounding cities and even out of province hoping I had connections in their area for a service like mine. One of my clients even approached me twice to take on the role as Property Manager for their whole complex along with a few others who couldn't find commercial property managers they were comfortable with. I was not experienced enough with the budgeting of commercial properties and knew that would definitely require licensing plus I was most certainly not interested in sitting in on never ending condo board meetings.

It was a real ego boost to be in great demand like this and another sign of success when I realized that I could pick and choose the kinds of properties and clients I took on now. I no longer felt obligated to accept properties that I already learned would be high maintenance or were in less than desirable neighbourhoods. I earned the ability to cherry pick but, I was definitely going to need help if I no longer wanted to turn away the good ones.

It required a very high level of organization to maintain correspondence between all these tenants and different owners who lived all over the world and different condo boards and service repair contractors and trades on top of managing my role as a mother, chauffeur, pet owner, housekeeper, yard care worker, bill payer, garbage take outer, daughter, sister, friend, neighbour…I was burning that midnight oil right to the end of my wick and knew I had to adjust my business plan. I just wasn't sure how.

My business model wouldn't work as smoothly for clients or me if it became broken by delegating parts of it out to hired help. I did not want my clients talking to an answering service that could never answer their questions. I was not really interested in managing many staff as I knew that I would still be called upon while trying to relax on vacation. I needed to be able to take real breaks without demands from tenants, clients, or staff. My business model worked for small business but it was difficult to envision growing it large enough by myself to a point where it would be feasible to hire office staff.

I had to find people who were just as entrepreneurial and organized as I was who were willing to show a property one day and scrub it clean the next day and be detail oriented enough to handle paperwork. People that I would not have to hand hold while I was sipping cocktails on a beach, somewhere. These people would have to duplicate exactly what I did.

The Anderson Career Training Institute offered ongoing support to graduates of the program and they met with me to strategize a way to hire out sub contracted help without the messiness of government deductions and paperwork and benefits for actual "employees". I placed a tester ad on my Facebook page and found two trusted acquaintances that I thought could handle replicating exactly what I was doing. Each one lived in the different far away corners of Edmonton that I was struggling to service efficiently by myself. One of these trusted associates was trained in interior design and was a perfect complement for enhancing rental properties. I had gone to high school with her and knew that she was very detail oriented and operated with the same integrity I did.

The other associate was a licensed realtor and was perfect for handling those realtor questions that my clients had. It was exactly what Sly Solutions Ltd needed to enhance credibility on all levels and grow even bigger.

There was a learning curve to get over of course. Tenants and clients were still calling me when they could not reach their agent and the subcontracted agents had to contact me on most transactions until they became more familiar with the landlord and tenant laws. No pain, no gain. Right?

CHAPTER 7
Sweet Success

The minute I added their credential information in interior design and real estate background to my website I was getting calls from clients with luxury homes, not just simply executive, but luxury. I had clients willing to pay the highest of rates and trusting me based on my knowledge, professionalism, experience, my A+ BBB rating and the fact that there was not any black mark found on line anywhere against my services, and of course because there was no risk.

Within two years of incorporating and marketing my business and within six months of hiring subcontracted help I grew to over $100,000 in revenue from the residual income of full management on approximately 50-60 properties plus my extended services of cleaning, restoration, and tenant placements. I had arrived. Finally.

After struggling for so many years to make ends meet I didn't feel desperate for a boyfriend or a roommate anymore. The banker in me was always a good financial budgeter, but I no longer had to choose only groceries that were on sale or limit myself to buying clothes for me and my daughter at Walmart. Living in an affluent community like St. Albert can have an effect on a young girl's self-esteem who isn't adorned with the same Lululemon outfits everyone else is flaunting. Although I was proud that my daughter was not materialistic, it was comforting to just be able to afford the luxury stuff.

I could afford to travel without using only accumulated travel reward points and I could afford to bring my daughter with me. I didn't have to worry anymore about the cost of gas while travelling to visit my parents and brother in Lac La Biche. I could contribute more to my daughter's RESP for the university education she was already deserving of as an honour student at 12 years old. I no longer had to sacrifice haircuts for myself to afford her music and dance lessons that she was a natural at. I was able to go to the salon more than three times per year now. I could even afford fancy nails. I was no longer worried about how I would make ends meet once my daughter was grown and I would no longer be receiving child support payments. I felt so free and empowered and proud of my achievements.

I had built a successful and reputable business based on a strong foundation of ethical principles in helping landlords and tenants.

It was difficult for me to step back and not act like a boss because I was not a boss. They were subcontractors, not actual employees. It was still my business name attached to these two subcontractors and I was trying to guide them in performing the way I performed. That old saying "if you want something done right, do it yourself" kept rearing itself in my mind but if I was going to build up this landlord agent business to the point of having others work it while I managed it from a beach someday, I was going to have to get through the growing curve.

The creative juices sloshed through my mind as I wondered how I could capitalize on this business without doing all the day to day work myself and not constantly be at someone's beck and call.

And then it hit me. Franchise! That was the golden word. The vision of packaging all my template forms and website and marketing materials and experience to build manuals outlining processes and resources to sell as a Landlord Agent business start-up package and branded under Sly Solutions Ltd. Brilliant! Selling the model to entrepreneurs just like me. Beautiful.

I did not have the time to do that though. Yet. I believed I could do it and that I would do it though. I had to.

I never intended to ever have a dissatisfied client. Getting a black mark on my Better Business Bureau A+ rating was the last thing I expected to bring my business crashing down. Yet, although I have never had a client file a complaint regarding any of my services, the universe did bring a surprising twist to my success and it ruined my life just as quickly as it had once improved…

CHAPTER 8
To Sell or Not To Sell...?

In July 2012 I received a call from my instructor and mentor at Anderson Career Training Institute regarding an ad he had seen on Kijiji from Libertas Property Management looking to buy out rental portfolios. After our strategizing meeting, he thought I might be interested in selling my business so passed the information on to me. I appreciated that thoughtfulness and it reinforced the value of that program. The timing had been perfect for me to consider selling as I was so full of stress from the latest mishaps I encountered with one of my executive homes in St. Albert.

One of my clients, who had moved to Australia, was refusing to pay the roofing company the $15,000 for the new tar and gravel roof work that was agreed upon by him and coordinated by me. The roofing company was threatening to sue me and the long trail of bad luck that preceded and followed this "Monster Mansion" property was threatening my sanity. Having to deal with the growing curve with my subcontracted associates on top of it was bringing me to the edge of a cliff questioning how long I could handle this daily unescapable stress from occurrences that seemed out of my control.

I called the number in the ad for Libertas Property Management and spoke with Carolyn Hackett to inquire about what would be involved in selling a portfolio like mine. Of course she asked how many properties I had and where they were located, what kind of properties, how big was the rent roll, etc. The fact that I did not hold the "rent roll" made it difficult to determine the value of the business in my mind and the fact that my clients hired me so they could handle their own "rent roll" made me realize that selling my portfolio to them would be a complicated process. I would be selling my client list only and that would be breaking confidentiality agreements. Carolyn admitted that her company would not offer the option for owners to receive rents directly. If I asked permission, most of my clients would choose not to transfer their business to a property management company holding their rent in trust accounts. I obviously needed to consider this a little further before making any decisions.

This was not a million dollar business either, yet, so I also needed to consider other career options to replace this landlord agent one before jumping ship.

That lead me to the same head banging against the wall that I faced before I settled on being a landlord agent. Even though my daughter was older now and not requiring a babysitter anymore, she still needed me to drive her to dance lessons and music lessons and no job out there would provide the perfect hours to allow me to be home in time after work to do that. If I could have come up with a better business idea I would have done it already.

As disenchanted as I was with the negative energy that came with managing tenants, it provided the financial stability I needed and the ability to schedule my own work hours. It gave me freedom. I decided that if I could just rid myself of the high maintenance properties and only take on the higher profit luxury homes then I could carve out a new niche and not have to dabble in cleaning and renovations anymore. So I put on my big girl panties determined to do just that.

It had only been two weeks since I had first chatted with Carolyn Hackett of Libertas Property Management when she called me up trying to convince me to sell. She had closely reviewed my website and was excited to see all the St. Albert executive homes on my sample portfolio page. She also lived in St. Albert. Really? It was interesting to also learn from her that she was familiar with the realtor associate, Moe, who I showcased on my website.

She claimed she knew Moe from their latest portfolio acquisition from the real estate brokerage he was licensed under. Very interesting information indeed and should be noted to remember in future chapters.

I explained to her again that my business model was too different from theirs making it difficult to put a fair sale value on it and that my clients appreciated managing their own rent money. I assured her that if and when I was seriously ready to sell, I would contact her.

Carolyn poked me a few more times with email follow ups and phone calls proving to be very eager to purchase my lucrative portfolio list. She even offered a payment plan option "if that would benefit my tax situation." It wasn't my tax situation I was concerned about.

I have copied the first email correspondence here and you will find further email correspondence between Carolyn and myself as we go along in future chapters in their date order. The timing of these emails from her are evidence of collaborated extortion.

From: "Carolyn Hackett" <carolyn@lpmimgmt.com>
Date: November 27, 2012 10:40 PM
To: <sylvia@slysolutions.ca>
Subject: Property Management- Selling

Hi Sylvia- hope all is well. Just thought I would touch base again to see if you have made any decisions about selling your business.

Regards,
Carolyn Hackett, B.B.A
Landlord Liason/REALTOR

LIBERTAS
Property Management Inc.

Looking to buy an investment property? Have one of our REALTORS help you and receive 6 months of free property management! Ask us for more details.

Libertas Property Management Inc.
10612-178 Street, Edmonton, AB T5S 2E3
Office: 780.478.6492 Ext. 801
Fax: 780.406.2892
Camrose: 780.679.0002
www.LPMImgmt.com
www.RentAlberta.Info

2016-09-28

She seemed determined to do whatever she could to convince me to sell. After months of me saying "No" to her, I was going to learn just how determined she really was and 5 months after I approached her about her Kijiji ad, I got the phone call that would change the course of my life.

SECTION II

Bully Alert

> *"Beware of false prophets who come to you in sheep's clothing but inwardly are ravenous wolves."*
> **-Anonymous**

CHAPTER 9
The Start of the End

I was not familiar with the Real Estate Council of Alberta (RECA) when Sherry Hillas called me on January 10, 2013. How would I be? I was not a realtor and never had the need to be familiar with them. I first thought that this was a telemarketing call to promote benefits of membership just as BBB approached me. Well, I was so wrong.

RECA had somehow become familiar with me based on an "anonymous complaint" they had received and they had some questions about my business operations. Anonymous complaint? My naivety had me initially thinking that the roofing company who threatened to sue me 6 months earlier had complained but I knew that I was not legally liable for that roof work based on my client contracts.

Sherry Hillas would not divulge when this complaint came in or who it was from. I believed I had nothing to hide so I chose to cooperate with explaining my business. The telephone questions however turned into more of an interrogation with the court room version of "yes" or "no" questions leaving no option for full explanations. For example "Do you show properties on behalf of the owner?" "Do you advertise properties on behalf of the owner?" "Do you negotiate lease agreements on behalf of the owner?" "Are you aware that you require a real estate license to show properties?"

Huh? Why on earth would I need to have a real estate license to show a renter a condo unit? I did not know of a single on-site condo manager that had a real estate license. They would be selling houses for much bigger money than the peanuts they were getting showing condo units. Seriously. This obviously had nothing to do with coordinating that roofing job. I felt like I was in some TV episode of Law and Order being coerced to admit some kind of guilt to a crime I didn't commit.

Of course I showed properties. That's typically what out of town owners need assistance with.

Of course I advertised the properties. Marketing was one of my strengths that my clients leaned on me for. Could you imagine a realtor expecting a seller to advertise on MLS themselves?! Of course not. That just does not make sense.

I did not "negotiate" leases or rent amounts. The rent on the ad was the rent that went on the lease. Every lease was the same with the same rules as I used pre-printed duplicate leases from ARLA (Alberta Residential Landlord Association). The only difference between one lease and another lease was the owner name and tenant name. Sherry responded to that explanation with "If you are signing the lease then you are negotiating it". What?! We must have been referring to different dictionaries to determine the true meaning of "negotiating". One of the many reasons my clients appreciated my work was because I did not "negotiate" rent amounts with tenants. The owners called the shots and I simply executed it. I did not negotiate it.

It was obviously a black/white game with no grey allowed but the fine line here was grey. Not quite 50 shades of grey but grey nonetheless.

When I started throwing my own questions at Sherry Hillas she proceeded to explain that she was new and would check with a higher up officer. It was her opinion though that I required a real estate license if I was advertising and showing properties. What the hell was this? Do not call to interrogate me if you do not wear the hat to arrest me.

I requested something in writing from her and she advised that I would be receiving a letter in the mail. Well, that would be the last time I ever answered a telephone call. All unknown calls started going to voicemail and still do today. If callers do not leave a detailed message, I do not call them.

On January 28, 2013 I received a Professional Conduct Review Letter in the mail in regards to "the receipt of information as of August 2, 2012 concerning the business activities of Sly Solutions Ltd".

REAL ESTATE
COUNCIL
OF ALBERTA®

Our Ref:	003228
Your Ref:	
Please ask for:	Sherry Hillis
Direct Dial:	403-685-7937
e-mail:	shillis@reca.ca

Private and Confidential

Sylvia Germain

████████████████

St. Albert, AB
T8N 6H8

January 24, 2013

Dear Ms. Germain

Notification of Commencement of a Professional Conduct Review Under the
Real Estate Act

The Real Estate Council of Alberta (RECA) is a self-regulatory organization responsible for the enforcement of the *Real Estate Act* (Act). Rules made pursuant to the *Real Estate Act* set standards of conduct for industry professionals to protect the public.

The executive director of the Real Estate Council of Alberta is appointed by the Council as the chief administrative officer of the Council.

As of August 2, 2012 the executive director is in receipt of information concern the activities of your business Sly Solutions Ltd.

Suite 350, 4954 Richard Road SW, Calgary, AB T3E 6L1 Telephone: (403) 228-2954 Fax: (403) 228-3065
003228/063328 Toll Free: 1-888-425-2754 Web site: www.reca.ca E-mail: info@reca.ca
Page 1 of 3

RECA conducts a professional conduct review (PCR) according to a formal process based on the requirements of the Act and the principles of natural justice (which promote fairness throughout the process).

RECA's process has three main objectives:

- to gather all relevant information to enable the executive director and hearing panels to make an informed decision on the facts of the matter under review
- to treat all parties courteously, fairly, impartially and according to the rules of administrative law
- to gather information in a timely and efficient manner

RECA's processes are designed to achieve these objectives with as little disruption as possible and consideration given to personal or business issues.

On or about January 10, 2013 during a telephone conversation with a Professional Conduct Review Officer, you indicated that you were negotiating the leases for rental units on behalf of your clients. This is an activity that is considered a trade in real estate as defined by the Act, and does require authorization.

The PCR will gather evidence to assist the executive director in determining whether you may have breached the Act or require authorization. To assist the executive director with this decision, please provide all information relevant to this matter including the following by **February 14, 2103:**

1. A copy of all transaction records and/or relevant documents held by Sly Solutions in relation to property management activities, including, but not limited to, all management agreements, leases, move in, move out reports, all correspondence with clients and/or service providers, advertising records, general ledger financial statements for the period of January 1, 2012 to the present time.

2. A detailed list of all Alberta clients including all contact information for the period of May 1, 2011 to the present time.

3. A listing of the services provided to clients in Alberta.

4. Your detailed written description of the process you follow with a new client.

5. Your detailed written description of the process you follow with a new tenant.

6. Do you collect a security deposit? Who holds that deposit? What advice do you give regarding the security deposit and its return?

Page 2 of 3

7. How do you advise your clients in terms of the lease? Do you explain each clause and term? How do you answer questions pertaining to the amount of rent that should be charged, or the terms of the lease?

8. How do you advise potential tenants in terms of the lease? Do you explain each clause and term? Do you answer questions pertaining to terms of the lease?

9. Who prepared your lease documents?

10. How do you get remunerated for your services?

11. Please provide any other information you feel may be relevant.

You may provide this information to RECA by email to shillis@reca.ca, by fax (403-228-3065) or by hard copy to the Real Estate Council of Alberta at Suite 350, 4954 Richard Road S.W. Calgary, Alberta, T3E 6L1. Please reference our case number noted at the top of this letter.

All information received will be subject to an in independent and unbiased evaluation. Upon completion of the review and if there is a need for further information you will receive notice in writing.

The time required to complete this review will depend on factors such as its complexity, the level of co-operation of all parties and the number of reviews underway.

I am employed by the Real Estate Council of Alberta as a conduct review officer. I have been appointed by the executive director of the Real Estate Council of Alberta to conduct a professional conduct review concerning your activities.

If you have any questions, please call me at 403-685-7937.

Yours truly,

Sherry Hillis
Professional Conduct Review Officer

Page 3 of 3

Was this for real? These requests were more outrageous than a CRA audit! Each of my client files was at least ¼" thick, some 1" thick and there were over fifty of those files. It was not feasible to copy all that paper especially in a two week period. Could you imagine the cost and time to do something like that? Who were they to demand confidential information like they were demanding?

They did not even divulge what the "information" they received was or who filed that "information" with them. Didn't I have a right to know that?

I wasn't even their industry member to push around like this. I was an independent contractor dealing with residential tenants. I was not selling real estate or managing commercial properties. I couldn't figure out what the big deal was and why they were so concerned about my little business. I knew I had not done anything wrong or unethical. I was helping people!

I called Moe, one of the new subcontractors I had hired on to assist me with tenant placements in the North East and South East corners of Edmonton. He was a licensed realtor so I expected he would be familiar with RECA and their level of power. It was with that phone call to Moe that I learned that RECA had been investigating his affiliation with Sly Solutions Ltd two months earlier. He didn't think to share that with me as he knew I was already overwhelmed with my workload and did not want to add any more stress on my plate. He advised me that RECA was concerned about the fact that he was showcased on my website appearing as though he was licensed under Sly Solutions Ltd as his licensing brokerage. Moe did not even question how they became aware of our affiliation but explained his role with Sly Solutions Ltd. He was given written clearance to remain working with me and being showcased as one of my affiliates on my website as long as his licensing brokerage was noted. **This is very important and interesting to remember because 3 years later RECA penalized him for exactly what they cleared him for at this time.**

Why did Sherry Hillas not mention anything to me about this specifically? Adding Moe's real estate licensing brokerage firm under his credentials on my website was only a five minute fix for me. Sherry Hillas had not been concerned about my website at all when interrogating me. If I was doing something so wrong why was Moe given the green light to continue working with me? This was not making any sense at all. Carolyn Hackett was already a common denominator.

CHAPTER 10
Legal Eagle Hunt

I was losing a lot of sleep over those next few days and was full of anxiety about how to deal with these intrusive demands. I was literally sick with mental anguish. My right shoulder had broken out in an ugly rash and I was feeling sharp stabbing pains up the right side of my torso. I went to see my Doctor at the Associate Medical Clinic in St. Albert. I'll never forget him saying to me "You must be under a lot of stress right now". I cried my response "Yup, you could say that". He diagnosed me with shingles and told me I caught it just in time to be able to nip it in the butt with antibiotics.

I have never in my life experienced stress to this degree; not even through my divorce. My family and friends were encouraging me not to worry about this so much and that RECA could not possibly have the right to invade my files without reason. I had witnessed enough red tape tug of war to know that the bad guy is always the bigger guy and can afford to win without even trying. I didn't know exactly what or who I was up against and it was obvious I needed legal counsel.

I scheduled a meeting with the lawyer that had assisted me with writing up my client contract during my entrepreneur business training at Anderson Career Training Institute and I trusted that she would advise me fairly.

During that free consultation with this lawyer on February 5, 2013, she did some quick research on line about RECA and their mandate and she advised me by simply quoting to me "you're not an industry member and therefore are not governed by them". That's exactly what I thought! I walked out of her office with a renewed sense of empowerment and could not wait to tell this Sherry Hillas how to shove it, in the most professional way of course.

In hindsight, I probably should not have answered any of their investigation questions but at that time I believed that it was important for this council to realize that I was not a threat to my clients. I was not portraying myself as one of their industry members. I thought I had it covered in the response letter that I forwarded on February 8, 2013 to Sherry Hillas.

February 8, 2013

Real Estate Council of Alberta
#350 4954 Richard Rd SW
Calgary, AB
T3E 6L1

ATTN: Sherry Hillas Ref # 003228

I can appreciate the need for a regulatory body to protect the public by following up on conduct for industry professionals however **I am not an industry member** and not privy to the governing rules and regulations in the Real Estate Act. I am not a realtor and I do not practice real estate transactions. I do not trade in real estate or provide sale advice, home sale values, rent-to-own options, or any advice related to trading in real estate. I do not attempt to act in the capacity of one of your industry members even when asked to by potential or existing clients. I refer my clients to a licensed realtor if they require real estate advice just as realtors refer property investors requiring tenant placement and management services to me AFTER the real estate deal is completed.

Before I comply with releasing documents that contain confidential client AND tenant information I have a right to be made aware of what this "matter under review" is pertaining to that was brought to your attention on August 2, 2012 that indicated I was infringing on the reputation of the real estate industry.

I also have a right to be made aware of any enforcing consequences should I not comply with the unreasonable requests made upon me in such a limited time period. It is not reasonable to approach me half a year after an August 2, 2012 "receipt of information" and still hold me liable for rules and regulations seven months after that period because you have refrained from bringing it to my attention in due time. It has been brought to my attention by Moe ██████,
a licensed realtor who I subcontract some of my work to and refer existing clients

to for sales advice, that RECA recently informed him that he was required to elaborate on his licensing credentials that I have advertised on my website. Fair enough. I was afraid that having that information on my website would be misconstrued as though I was also acting under that umbrella. I was not made aware myself by RECA of that requirement but I have taken my website down until I have that rectified. That certainly isn't a reasonable enough "infringement" to warrant such a full-fledged review of highly confidential information. I have not acted criminally and am confident that you do not hold any information to prove that I have. I would consider bringing any questionable files into your office for your review to prove the level of legal integrity that I work with but I cannot reasonably copy every piece of paper or email communication or note written in my folders for the time period requested and my accountant has all my financial statements for CRA purposes.

I have taken the appropriate measures to complete an approved Government sponsored entrepreneur training program and have been advised on how to operate my business within the law. My client contract was also reviewed by legal counsel.

The Alberta Residential Tenancies Act sets the guidelines that I use for my tenant placement and management services. My website (that has already been reviewed by you) indicates very clearly what services are provided by Sly Solutions Ltd and describes my background and story honestly. I do not present myself or my credentials falsely. I have been approached many times to manage both old and new apartment complexes because these boards could not find a good commercial property manager that would accept smaller scale complexes. I have been honest in my continuous refusal responses to take these on because I am not a licensed manager to handle contracts of that magnitude. I also do not provide mortgage advice even though I have been asked many times due to my previous mortgage lending experience noted on my website. I do not involve myself with commercial contracts.

I have a right to sell my own residential property without a licensed realtor. I also have a right to own and manage unlimited residential rental properties and negotiate unlimited leases and I have a right to pay anyone I choose to assist me with the management of this in whatever capacity I require. My clients have that same right. My services are in high demand for investment owners who don't feel comfortable with forms and standing up to tenants due to lack of knowledge, experience, or time. This public is at risk with tenants and share my belief that their risk is lessened by having services such as mine available to them. Many clients have come to me because they have been ripped off by licensed property managers who have not forwarded rents to them held in trust and these clients appreciate the fact that I do not operate in the same regard that licensing allows.

I do not advertise any properties falsely. (You might consider chasing the scammers that do duplicate my ads falsely at ½ the rent attempting to collect wired security deposits. Now that's a huge risk to the public!) I do not misrepresent client intentions to potential renters falsely just to secure a renter. I ensure that I understand my clients long term intentions for the property in order to match the right tenant. I do not tease potential clients with unrealistic rent values to gain new business. I go through a detailed spec sheet process with potential clients to help me compare to other advertised comparables that help me determine realistic rent values while keeping their actual bottom line costs in mind. I provide an email copy of my contract to all potential clients before visiting their property so that they are aware of how I do business before committing to hiring me. My contract is very detailed about my process and obligations of both the owner and Sly Solutions Ltd. I provide a triplicate copy of an invoice and an on line ad copy to all my clients for their review. My tenant placement fees are deducted from the cash balance I deposit from the 1st month's rent and detailed bank deposit slips are forwarded to owners. I do not hold security deposit or rent money in bank accounts so I do not earn interest income on either. They are held by the owner and are refunded by the owner directly to the tenant based on the refund statement I provide them. The zero % interest rate payable on security deposits over the last couple years should not even warrant any further concern in this area at this time.

All tenants are made aware, upon completing an application process, that cash is expected for security deposit as well as 1st month's rent with a triplicate cash receipt provided. Those cash receipts all have the owners/clients name on them and rental property address. Tenants provide post-dated rent cheques payable to that owner. Those post-dated rent cheques are mailed to the owner by me and they provide me with an equivalent number of post-dated cheques for monthly fees.

I follow through with all condo board new tenant notification requirements and pertinent condo by law package receipt by tenants.

I do not mark-up repair or maintenance services that are contracted out. I coordinate the service with the client's approval and the owner pays the service company directly.

I collaborate with owners about qualifying applications before any lease signing or renewal completion. The owners name is on all leases with my name and contact information and signature as Landlord Agent.

I use lease agreements provided by the Edmonton Apartment Association and receive updated and valuable information pertaining to landlords with my membership. It's in my best interest to clearly explain all lease clauses to tenants because I'm the one who deals with any aftermath. **These lease clauses are defined by the Residential Tenancies Act not the Real Estate Act.** I am not comfortable, nor obligated in providing a do-it-yourself step by step manual of the successful professional processes I follow with clients AND tenants to be infringed upon or duplicated by your industry members or anybody else without deserved recognition. I worked hard and paid my educational dues and received appropriate legal consultation to put my process together. I would be open though to collaborating with RECA on such an idea to get services such as mine recognized as an important one in protecting the public in the residential rental industry.

I act in the capacity of a personal assistant, a house sitter, a secretary, a cleaning lady, and a painter NOT a Real Estate industry member. My services are not required until AFTER the client finalizes their real estate deal. No level of understanding of real estate or mortgage brokerage can assist with the 24/7 on call position of receiving complaints, coordinating services, paperwork, and tenant baby-sitting. I am not making big easy money. It is an extremely stressful environment being the middle man agent dealing with so many different owners, tenants, condo boards, service companies, utility companies, banks, RTDRS, etc. and it requires exceptional organizational skills and the heart of a lion to do what I do and stay sane. I hate what I do but I do it because there is a demand for it and I do it successfully because of my work ethic and business background and it's the income I rely on to support my daughter. Trying to take me down will not be protecting the public as much as it would be inconveniencing them while destroying the mental and financial capacity of a single Mother to protect her child.

Sylvia Germain

HER MAJESTY, by and with the advice and consent of the Legislative Assembly of Alberta, enacts as follows:

Interpretation

1(1) In this Act,

    (a) "common areas" means areas controlled by a landlord and used for access to residential premises or for the service or enjoyment of tenants;

    (b) "council" means

        (i) the council of a city, town, village, municipal district or Metis settlement,

        (ii) in the case of an improvement district, the Minister determined under section 16 of the *Government Organization Act* as the Minister responsible for the *Municipal Government Act*, or

        (iii) in the case of a special area, the Minister determined under section 16 of the *Government Organization Act* as the Minister responsible for the *Special Areas Act*;

    (c) "court" means

        (i) the Provincial Court, or

        (ii) the Court of Queen's Bench;

    (d) "Director" means the Director of Residential Tenancies appointed under section 55;

    (e) "fixed term tenancy" means a tenancy under a residential tenancy agreement for a term that ends on a day specified in the agreement;

    (f) "landlord" means

        (i) the owner of the residential premises,

        (ii) a property manager who acts as agent for the owner of the residential premises and any other person who, as agent for the owner, permits the occupation of the residential premises under a residential tenancy agreement,

4

I really thought I had explained my business model very clearly and that I had also demonstrated my required level of knowledge of the law. The Real Estate Act did not govern my business activities as a Landlord Agent so RECA did not govern me. It seemed simple to me, as well as to anyone else outside of their industry.

I managed to get some sleep after sending that letter off believing that Sherry Hillas would actually read it and they would move onto more important regulatory matters.

*"Never hate people who are jealous of you. They're
people who think that you're better than them."*
-Anonymous

CHAPTER 11
The Cat Came Back
the Very Next Day

On February 11, 2013 I received another email from Carolyn Hackett of Libertas Property Management. She was again eager in wanting to offer me a lump sum for my portfolio. It was on this day that I realized Carolyn Hackett had been interested in my portfolio since July of 2012, the same time frame that RECA claimed to have been "in receipt of information regarding Sly Solutions Ltd business activities". I put two and two together.

Carolyn Hackett had obviously filed the 'anonymous' complaint with RECA in hopes that RECA would pressure me enough to decide to sell out to her in a desperate position. I did not appreciate the thought that someone could be that malicious, but considering the number of times in my life that I have been bullied or challenged because of others jealousy it did not surprise me.

From: Carolyn Hackett
Sent: Monday, February 11, 2013 1:51 PM
To: sylvia@slysolutions.ca
Subject: FW: Property Management- Selling

Hi Sylvia- Just wanted to touch base with you again regarding the sale of your business. Libertas is interested in acquisitions at this time. I know we talked briefly last year and you were not sure what your business was valued at and you were looking into having it appraised. Are you ready to sit down and now chat about a possible purchase? Libertas would be prepared to offer you a lump sum. Please advise.

Regards,
Carolyn Hackett, B.B.A
Landlord Liason/REALTOR

From: Sly Solutions [mailto:sylvia@slysolutions.ca]
Sent: February-12-13 9:07 AM
To: Carolyn Hackett
Subject: Re: Property Management- Selling

Hello Carolyn,

I can appreciate your interest in my portfolio however I must find a way to replace this income before I step out of what I worked so hard to achieve. I do have a daughter to support and it will take some time to either put together a new business idea that can replace this income or to find a 'job position' with an employer who will hire someone who has already been so independent as a business owner.

I will certainly look you up again when I have my ducks in a row.

Warm Regards,
Sylvia Germain,

Thank you for your quick response, when you are ready to chat, just let me know.

Regards,
Carolyn Hackett, B.B.A
Landlord Liason/REALTOR

When I responded to Carolyn's email I simply tried to make her realize that as a single mother, I needed to consider and secure another career or business option to replace this lucrative income before I could consider selling, and that I would look her up if ever I was ready for that. I honestly imagined that she might have enough nurturing female genes to give some consideration of my position. As time would tell, imagination is not reality.

CHAPTER 12
Daily Grind Grinds Me

I went about my daily grind as usual with continuous calls for showings and repairs that would weigh me down like a brick sinking in water. It still amazes me how poorly everything is made in this new age of technology. My house is twenty one years old at the time I'm writing this, and I have not experienced anywhere near the level of repair to my house as I've experienced with the majority of the properties in my portfolio, no matter how new or renovated they are. I still have the same furnace yet I've had to deal with furnace replacements in ten year old properties!

Kitchen appliances don't last any longer than that these days either. Plumbing fixtures only last two years now and aren't built to be repaired anymore, so you're forced to buy a whole new faucet and spend $300 with installation versus $60 to replace a part. Even though I updated my kitchen after fifteen years I still have the same kitchen faucet, and I refuse to replace it as long as it works.

Lighting fixtures are also crap these days and need frequent replacing because sockets just stop working. Tenants seem to be too lazy to even try and figure out how to replace a bulb in new fixtures today let alone try to find the right replacement bulb and spend the $9 for one bulb.

Every day, I'm bombarded with repair issues regarding electrical, lighting, toilets, faucets, shower heads, shower doors, fridges, stoves, microwaves, dishwashers, washers, dryers, garburators, bathroom fans, furnaces, humidifier floods, sewer back-ups, air conditioning, leaking roofs, leaking basements, sum pumps, doors jamming from foundation movement, chimneys, eaves troughs and downspouts, garage door sensors/openers/motors, plugged garage drains, door locks, cupboard hinges, central vacuums, closet shelves and hardware, windows, screens, gates, fences, blinds, curtain rod brackets falling out, towel bars falling out, hot tubs leaking, decks rotting, tree branches breaking, weed problems, freezing pipes, burst pipes, fires...

Those are just *some* of the regular repair issues, not to mention the other management issues like rent cheque problems, utility issues, thefts, condo board complaints and maintenance, co-ordinating yard care and snow removal, insurance claims, neighbour and bylaw complaints, pets, advertising properties for rent, screening renters tenant sign - ins, leases, lease renewals, inspections, rents, tenant sign outs, evictions, cleaning, painting, renovating, security deposit refund statements and tenants fighting to not be accountable for damages and cleaning, court hearings, client communications and approvals for repairs book keeping, invoicing, banking, tax statements, photocopying and mailing, driving and more driving, etc...

For a one woman show I think I did a remarkable job holding everything together and getting 'er done expediently with organized mania on or before schedule. Maintaining my own corner lot on top of that with 15 deciduous trees had me crying in my piles of leaves. I kept waiting for that gold star of service but there wasn't anybody above me to give me one!

Many of my clients praised me and that was much appreciated. However that praise did not ease the day to day demands on me.

I really did not love the stress and negativity attached to this industry, and my role particularly, and I wished upon that star that I could sell my portfolio but I did not even have an undisturbed moment to be able to dream up a new income opportunity. I am also a very stubborn woman sometimes and there was no way in hell I was going to let a malicious person such as Carolyn Hackett of Libertas Property Management get the portfolio I burned myself out over with real blood, sweat, and tears for just a simple money transfer that still wouldn't be enough for me to retire in the Caribbean. If she wanted a lucrative portfolio like mine she was going to have to work just as hard as I did.

CHAPTER 13
Cease and Desist

A couple weeks had gone by since I had sent my response letter. On February 27, 2013 I had come home from another long day of driving for month end sign out inspections to a voicemail on my home office phone from a different RECA gal named Robin Barron asking me to call her. I figured this must be the higher up gal that Sherry Hillas referred to, and she was just going to have to wait a few days until month end had passed.

The next day, February 28, 2013 I received another voicemail from an impatient sounding Robin Barron to call her immediately. She obviously did not have any realization that month end is an extremely hectic time for a Landlord Agent managing over fifty properties, especially ones that were spread across two different cities. My intention was to call her back after I had completed my priority work for my clients and that would be around the 5th of March.

Robin obviously could not wait a few days for me to return her call and on March 4, 2013 I had received another voicemail from her. This one stating she had determined that I was definitely trading in real estate and ordered me to cease and desist all business activities immediately and if I had not done so by March 25, 2013 I would face a $25,000 fine. Who the hell was this gal? Giving me an order like this by telephone message? I was enraged and sick to my stomach that this could be happening to me. I was not doing anything wrong and I had been helping these owners for over ten years already without any complaint. $25,000 fine?!

Although I knew I was not doing anything wrong, it was becoming apparent that this RECA organization was obviously determined to prove that I was. I felt backed up against a brick wall and had no idea what to do. These business activities were my bread and butter and I certainly was not about to cut my only income supply off by cancelling all my contracts with my present clients.

I felt scared and very uncertain about what I was up against and on March 5, 2013 decided to deactivate my website marketing on Rentfaster. ca and not accept any more new clients until seeking further legal counsel. I also put a freeze on my Vistaprint website www.slysolutions.ca and began looking for the biggest dog to fight back with.

SECTION III

In the Monopoly Ring

Part 1

Fight #1 - File #003228

CHAPTER 14
A Park Place Lawyer

I spent the next week burning up the internet looking for other legal opinions. I started with real estate lawyers and after three turned me down due to "conflict of interest" I finally learned that I needed to speak with someone who specialized in regulatory law. I found a couple regulatory lawyers that I left voice messages with and then I came across Miller Thomson Law office in downtown Edmonton that made my spidey senses tingle. I was impressed with their large North American presence and the credentials of the lawyers and the big dogs they have successfully gone up against. I trusted I would get the right advice here.

I could hardly believe my luck when one of them answered his phone and listened with interest to my explanation of receiving such intrusive demands from a regulatory council that did not govern me. He wanted to see this conduct review letter and my files to really understand what my business model was and invited me to share more in a free one hour consultation the following week. Perfect.

Later that day the two other lawyers I had left voice messages for had returned my call. I explained that I already arranged council with so and so of Miller Thomson and it was very encouraging to hear both of these lawyers commend me on getting through to the best lawyer in the city for this case. I was assured by both of them that he was a good honest gem and would take good care of me. The synchronicity really showed up when I shared this with my best friend Lynda that evening. She reacted with her Tigger energy about how she worked in his office for fifteen years before getting into massage therapy and that he was the most honest and genuine lawyer. Wow! Really? I found the golden legal eagle! It was about time I had some good luck.

On March 12, 2013 I arrived at Miller Thomson downtown law office at Commerce Place loaded with an armful of files to prove that I was running a legitimate, transparent and risk free service to my clients. During my elevator ride to the 27th floor it dawned on me that I was headed to probably the most prestigious law firm in the City of Edmonton and I agonized over how little old me wound up being in a position to require this level of legal assistance when I had done everything right by my clients and any higher power watching over me. Upon entering the double doors of this firm and seeing half of the City of Edmonton and its horizon I knew this level of prestige was going to cost big time and I had to make this hour count.

He reviewed some of my files and contracts and procedures and agreed that my business activities reflected those of an on-site manager. On-site managers were exempt from requiring a real estate license and considering there was not a true breach and there were no complaints against my business in ten years he determined that he should be able to make a simple phone call to Robin Baron, at no charge to me, and explain that this was not a case to be concerned with or to drag through a costly court process. You cannot imagine how grateful I was to hear that it could be that simple because based on the view from this office and being on the 27th floor I knew I would not be able to afford him. He agreed it was unreasonable to threaten me with cease and desist orders over the telephone and that they were using scare tactics to bully me and see how far they could push me. The thought racing through my mind at that moment was, "I'll show them…"

CHAPTER 15
I Got a New Girl Now, Again!

After my meeting with my Park Place lawyer I continued my day to day drudgery dealing with ongoing tenant and property issues and new client dealings. Clients were still being referred to me and I had no reason to turn away the new business that I assessed as profitable quality contracts.

On March 26, 2013, a couple weeks after meeting with Brian, I received a phone call from him regarding the run around he received in his attempts to contact RECA. Sherry Hillas, who signed off on the Professional Conduct Review letter I had received, bounced him over to Robin Baron. Robin Baron was the other conduct review officer who had bombarded me with "cease and desist" voice message orders. Robin Baron would not accept his call and bounced it to yet another conduct review officer, Tricia Hickey. It is said that Tricia Hickey claimed "that their bark was much worse than their bite" and that they would lay off their threats if I would call her to answer their questions.

Well, first off, I already answered their questions in great detail in my written letter response to Sherry Hillas on February 8, 2013 as well as verbally in Sherry's initial telephone ambush call on January 10, 2013. How many others was I going to have to explain myself to?

Second, RECA had not provided me with their reasoning for instigating this conduct review in the first place. There was no client or tenant complaint that I was being asked to provide defense explanation for. The only information I had not divulged to them was my client list and files and they had no right to that private information if I was not their industry member.

I expressed to my lawyer that I was not comfortable with another pointless telephone interrogation from yet another review officer because I could tell at this point that their intent was to harass and coerce versus "question" me, and based on their own unprofessional conduct thus far I was obviously not innocent until proven guilty. They had already deemed me guilty with their "cease and desist" orders.

My lawyer advised me to have the discussion with Tricia Hickey as she seemed to be open to working this out with me which would be cheaper than having him do it. I was already sick to my stomach just thinking about having to do this again. I knew she would not be as sweet with me as she seemed to have been with my lawyer.

I called Tricia Hickey that same day and of course she interrogated me with the exact same "yes" or "no" questions I had already answered with Sherry Hillas and was very taunting without any real interest in my answers.

I naturally was getting very agitated by her lack of empathy and asked her to review my initial response letter of February 8, 2013 that explained my business practices to be that of an on-site manager. She claimed she was not aware of that letter and that she would call me again after reviewing it. ARE YOU FUCKING KIDDING ME?! How could she not be aware of that letter? Was it common practice for this organization to demand such proprietary information and then just ignore the information provided?! I had been out of office politics for a long time but was this really the norm these days? It sounded to me like they needed some organizational training. I did not look forward to another follow up call.

CHAPTER 16
Smells like Extortion

Ten more frustrating days went by after my phone call to Tricia Hickey and I received an email on April 4, 2013 from Carolyn Hackett of Libertas Property Management. She was making another attempt, very late in the evening, to work out a payment plan with me for the purchase of my portfolio. She admitted it would be convenient for her and her partner to meet me for coffee right in St. Albert, as they both lived in St. Albert as well. How coincidental was that? It's no wonder she was so obsessed with my portfolio knowing that my website showcased numerous profitable executive rental homes that were also in St. Albert.

2013-04-04   10:16 PM

Hi there- I just wanted to follow up again as my partner and I were talking about your business as of late. We are wondering if we can work out some sort of monthly payout in order to help you move into your next career without big changes in cash flow. We would love the opportunity to grab a coffee with you sometime to discuss it further. We live in St. Albert also so we could easily meet one night to discuss. Please let me know.

Regards,
Carolyn Hackett, B.B.A
Landlord Liason/REALTOR

How sweet of her to consider my cash flow. It was not just coincidental that my first discussion with Carolyn Hackett about my portfolio was back in July/August 2012, the same date that was noted in RECA's Professional Conduct Review Letter on January 24, 2013. That letter stated "As of August 2, 2012 the executive director is in receipt of information concerning the activities of your business Sly Solutions Ltd."

The letter never divulged where this information came from or what the actual complaint or information was. Let us also remember how familiar Carolyn Hackett was with who Moe, was on my website, and the fact that RECA approached Moe at least two months before ever bothering me directly.

The telephone and email/letter trail wreaked with evidence that Carolyn Hackett advised RECA of my business in the hopes that they would put enough pressure on me that I would buckle and pass my portfolio onto her and remove the competition. **That is extortion. Last I heard and read extortion is illegal, even in Canada.**

No wonder RECA was demanding *all* of my personal client files as opposed to just a few. RECA was not concerned with any risk to the public, they just wanted my client list to pass onto Carolyn Hackett. Well, nobody was going to get my client list and I sure as hell was not going to sell out to Carolyn Hackett no matter how tough it got. Carolyn would have to earn her own portfolio the right way, just like I did, with hard work and integrity.

I did not respond to her email and I braced myself for the antagonizing phone call I knew I would undoubtedly soon get from Tricia Hickey.

The Reiki and massage treatment I took the time out for helped for a couple days until I did receive the dreaded follow up call from Tricia Hickey on April 25, 2013.

She was sticking to her power trip that I was definitely trading in real estate and the law was that I "needed to be a licensed broker and industry member in order to show or advertise a rental property." I was expected to get licensed or cease and desist or face a $25,000 fine. Who the hell was this woman to be telling me what the law is? I was an independent contractor and she was not a government or police official. It was going to be a cold day in hell before I became licensed with a group of mean girls like this.

I attempted to reason with her again with the fact that I do not sell properties or earn income from the sale of properties. I was simply a landlord agent whose activities were those of an on-site manager, and I deserved to be considered exempt from licensing. She argued that I would have to live on-site at a complex. Bullshit!!!! I dealt with many "on-site" managers who managed multiple buildings within different complexes. There were many times I had to schedule appointments at specific times to meet with these "on-site" managers to collect security book an elevator time for moving at least two weeks in advance because the "on-site" manager had so many buildings to juggle. How could this even be considered a reasonable cause to destroy me and my business?!

I scrambled again to explain that I did not hold security deposits or rent money. My clients hired me specifically for that reason and becoming a licensed broker would mean that I would be expected to hold money in trust and practice the same business model as their industry. My clients were looking for *my* services specifically to allow them full control of their rental income, not the service of brokerage firms that would control their rental income. I even planted the seed regarding my reason for not entering further sale discussions with Carolyn Hackett of Libertas Property Management in that I DID NOT HAVE A PORTFOLIO CASH BALANCE, ONLY A CLIENT LIST. Tricia ignored that statement and would not waiver.

I felt like this woman had some personal vendetta against me and believed that she was holding a much bigger crown than me or something. I had experienced many acts of jealousy against me since I was 12 years old when I blossomed bigger than the other girls. I had dealt with jealous wives both as a landlord agent and as a personal banker because of my natural DD cups and social personality. The attacks by these three different women at RECA was bringing up old memories of being bullied in high school and it was getting harder to breathe.

I demanded that she explain to me what the reasonable cause was for RECA to demand that I cease a reputable business that was my bread and butter, as a single mother, if there was not even a public concern or real complaint. I got the usual reply that I am not allowed to trade in real estate without proper licensing. When I questioned her on what they expected I was supposed to do for income if I just cancelled all my client contracts midterm, she laughed at me saying "that's not my problem". The reality is, my business was not their problem either. It was Carolyn Hackett's problem.

That is when I decided to let her know that I knew Carolyn Hackett of Libertas Property Management had instigated this investigation review and that I was clearly being coerced and extorted. Tricia claimed that RECA had just fluked upon my website and I called bullshit on that because my website had been very actively advertised on www.Rentedmonton.com and www.rentfaster.ca for three years already. Let me just note here as well that Carolyn Hackett refrained from contacting me again. Coincidence? What do *you* think?

When I advised her that I had done my research and knew that many realtors and other independent landlord agents were doing exactly what I was doing (maybe just not as effectively) she admitted that RECA was beginning to "crack down" on people "like me." People "like me" protected residential property owners from people like Carolyn Hackett. I refused to continue anymore telephone discussions with her and advised her to serve me her cease and desist order in writing to present to my lawyer and hung up.

A google search of Libertas Property Management showed 43 reviews on YELP that were mostly negative. Some of them referred to Carolyn Hackett specifically. Go figure.

"The more laws, the less justice."
-Anonymous

CHAPTER 17
Go Directly to Jail, Do Not Pass Go, Do Not Collect $200

The very next day, on April 26, 2013, I received an email "Cease and desist" order letter from Tricia Hickey that promised to bother me with another follow up in two weeks. I never did receive an original hard copy letter in the mail which I thought to be professionally inappropriate for such an order and the email attachment is copied here…

REAL ESTATE
COUNCIL
OF ALBERTA ®

Our Ref: 003228
Your Ref:
Please ask for: Tricia Hickey
Direct Dial: 403-685-7942
e-mail: thickey@reca.ca

Private and Confidential

Sylvia Germain
Sly Solutions Ltd.
St. Albert, AB
sylvia@slysolutions.ca

April 26, 2013

Dear Ms. Germain:

Unauthorized Trading in Real Estate as a Real Estate Broker Pursuant to Section 17 of the *Real Estate Act*

Based on the information gathered, the Real Estate Council of Alberta (RECA) has determined the activities that you perform for your business require a licence to trade in real estate in the province of Alberta. Evidence indicates the following:

1. You advertise properties on behalf of clients and the contact information provided in the advertisements is your name. This activity indicates that you trade as a real estate broker according to section 1(x)(iii) and 1(x)(v) of the Act.

2. You show the property to potential tenants on behalf of the owner and answer questions the tenant may have in regards to the property. This activity indicates that you trade as a real estate broker according to section 1(x)(iii) of the Act.

3. You are hired by the owner to help facilitate the process of obtaining tenants to enter into a lease. You continue to facilitate the relationship between the tenant and the owner by acting as a "middle man". This activity indicates that you trade as a real estate broker according to section 1(x)(viii) of the Act.

Suite 350, 4954 Richard Road SW, Calgary, AB T3E 6L1 Telephone: (403) 228-2954 Fax: (403) 228-3065
Toll Free: 1-888-425-2754 Web site: www.reca.ca E-mail: info@reca.ca

The *Real Estate Act* can be found online at www.reca.ca. Sections of the Act you may want to review are provided below and define what constitutes a trade for the purposes of real estate, property management and sale. Also enclosed with this letter is a news bulletin outlining what is considered "Holding oneself out".

(x) "trade" includes any of the following:

  (i)   a disposition or acquisition of, or transaction in, real estate by purchase or sale;

  (ii)   an offer to purchase or sell real estate;

  (iii)   an offering, advertisement, listing or showing of real estate for purchase or sale;

  (iv)   property management;

  (v)   holding oneself out as trading in real estate;

  (vi)   the solicitation, negotiation or obtaining of a contract, agreement or any arrangement for an activity referred to in subclauses (i) to (v);

  (vii)   collecting, or offering or attempting to collect, on behalf of the owner or other person in charge of real estate, money payable as

   (A)   rent for the use of the real estate, or

   (B)   contributions for the control, management or administration of the real estate;

  (viii)   any conduct or act in furtherance or attempted furtherance of an activity referred to in subclauses (i) to (vii).

(s.1) "property management" includes any of the following:

   (i)   leasing or offering to lease real estate or negotiating or approving, or offering to negotiate or approve, a lease or rental of real estate;

   (ii)   holding money received in connection with an activity referred to in subclause (i);

   (iii)   advertising, negotiating or carrying out any other activity, directly or indirectly, for the purpose of furthering an activity referred to in subclause (i) or (ii);

(w.01) "sale", in respect of real estate, includes an exchange, an option, a lease or any other disposition of an interest in real estate;

Additionally, I have enclosed a copy of further relevant legislation that applies to these circumstances – specifically:

- Section 1(1)(v) of the *Real Estate Act*, which defines "real estate broker";
- Section 17, which describes the authorization required; and
- Section 81, which outlines the consequences of trading without authorization.

(v) "real estate broker" means

    (i)   a person who, for another or others and for consideration or other compensation, either alone or through one or more persons, trades in real estate, or

    (ii)   a person who holds out that the person is a person referred to in subclause (i);

17 No person shall

  (a) trade in real estate as a real estate broker,

  (b) deal as a mortgage broker,

  (c) act as a real estate appraiser, or

  (d) advertise himself or herself as, or in any way hold himself or herself out as, a mortgage broker, real estate broker or real estate appraiser

unless that person holds the appropriate authorization for that purpose issued by the Council.

(x) "trade" includes any of the following:

  (i)   a disposition or acquisition of, or transaction in, real estate by purchase or sale;

  (ii) an offer to purchase or sell real estate;

  (iii) an offering, advertisement, listing or showing of real estate for purchase or sale;

  (iv) property management;

  (v) holding oneself out as trading in real estate;

  (vi) the solicitation, negotiation or obtaining of a contract, agreement or any arrangement for an activity referred to in subclauses (i) to (v);

  (vii) collecting, or offering or attempting to collect, on behalf of the owner or other person in charge of real estate, money payable as

    (A) rent for the use of the real estate, or

    (B) contributions for the control, management or administration of the real estate;

  (viii) any conduct or act in furtherance or attempted furtherance of an activity referred to in subclauses (i) to (vii).

81(1) A person who contravenes section 10(2), 17, 18(1), (2) or (3), 19, 20(2), (3), (4) or (5), 24(1)(a), 25(1), (2), (3), (5) or (9), 38(4)(a) or (4.1), 69(2), 73(2), 74(2) or 83.2(7) is guilty of an offence and liable to a fine of not more than $25 000.

(1.1) A person who fails to comply with an order issued under section 83.2 is guilty of an offence and liable to a fine of not more than $25 000.

(2) Where a corporation commits an offence under this Act, any officer, director or agent of the corporation who directed, authorized, acquiesced in, assented to or participated in the commission of the offence is guilty of the offence and is liable to the penalty under subsection (1), whether or not the corporation has been prosecuted for or convicted of the offence.

(3) A person who is convicted of an offence under section 17, 18, 20, 24 or 25 shall, in addition to any fine or penalty payable under this section or section 83, return all commissions and other remuneration received by that person in respect of the activity that constituted the offence.

(4) A prosecution under this Act may be commenced within 3 years after the date on which the offence is alleged to have been committed, but not after that date.

Given you were unaware your activities required a licence to trade in real estate in the province of Alberta, and you still do not believe you are required to hold a licence, the Executive Director has chosen to allow you two weeks, from today's date, to speak with a lawyer regarding this matter.

On Friday, May 10, 2013, RECA will contact you to ensure you are not trading in real estate without the required authorization under the *Real Estate Act*.

This is a reminder that you are not authorized to trade in real estate as a real estate broker in the province of Alberta. You are expected to refrain from all real estate broker activities until you become authorized by RECA.

If you have any questions, please do not hesitate to contact Tricia Hickey, Professional Conduct Review Officer, directly at 403-685-7942.

Yours truly,

Bob Myroniuk,
Executive Director

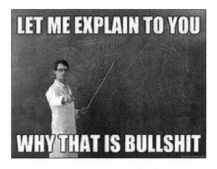

So, let's break this letter down a bit…

1) *"Based on the information gathered"* – Hmmm…the information I provided actually very clearly indicated that I was not trading in real estate. It was very clear that I was a residential landlord agent/ property manager that specialized in securing quality tenants with a distinctly different service than licensed property managers. It was clear that I did not control their money. It was also questionable as to who else they were gathering information from…?

2) Bullets 1, 2, and 3 refer to activities that any property owner can perform without a level of education. These are all also activities that "on-site" managers perform but do not require a broker license or any license for that matter, not even a realtor license.

3) On page 2, *(x) "trade" includes… (iv) property management* – At the time the Real Estate Act was written I can assume that "property management" was deemed to be management of apartment complexes and commercial property, not individually condominium units. The typical property manager at this time was not commonly managing individual residential units for individual investors until after the Alberta oil boom that had investors converting apartment complexes to condominium complexes. Regardless, Section 17 of the Real Estate Act authorizes RECA to regulate real estate brokers, mortgage brokers, and real estate appraisers. This section 17 DOES NOT INCLUDE property managers.

4) *(s.1) "property management" includes any of the following:*
Activity *(ii) holding money received in connection with an activity referred to in subclause (i)* – this cannot stand on its own and must be connected to either activity (i) and/or (iii). However, both activities (i) and (iii) CAN be performed without activity (ii). I do not perform activity (ii) and it is that activity that presents the risk to the public that is RECA's mandate to protect. My client contracts specifically state that all rent money I collect is by cheques payable to the owner, not payable to Sly Solutions Ltd. There is little or no risk to the property owner and therefore not a regulatory concern of this magnitude. This is the golden nugget of my business model. It's what sets me apart from the industry.

5) The last page reminds me *"to refrain from all real estate broker activities until I become licensed by RECA"* – What are broker activities? The three activities listed on the first page are on site manager activities, right? I had never acted or portrayed myself to be a real estate broker! My website portrayed me as a Landlord Agent/Property Manager and described my 13 years of marketing and lending experience in the banking industry thereby proficient in placing rental ads and screening tenants. The two subcontractors that I paid fees to did not work *for* me, they worked *with* me. They did not pay me brokerage fees. They were independent contractors performing the exact same activities as I was and I got paid 'finders fees' for securing the client contracts. This is perfectly legal. Realtors commonly pay 'finders fees' to others who bring them business.

It was obvious to me that nobody in this RECA office was reading my response letter from February 8, 2013 because they really did not care about my answers. They just wanted a piece of my pie.

"The woman who follows the crowd will usually go no further than the crowd. The woman who walks alone is likely to find herself in places no one has ever been before."
-Albert Einstein

CHAPTER 18
Why Not Get Licensed?

I forwarded the email to my lawyer and reiterated my discussion with Tricia Hickey. He could not understand why they were pushing it this far but did not seem to want to explore the idea of extortion. Probably because he knew it would be too costly for me to consider the court action attached to that. RECA obviously would not expect that I could be in a position to stand up against them either but they did not know who they were messing with.

My lawyer kept questioning me why I did not want to just get a real estate license and go bigger and get them off my back. Almost everybody has questioned me on that. That might be what a lot of other people might do but I saw through what would happen if I did.

The clear line in the sand here is this: If I was a licensed member I would not be allowed to provide the protective and transparent service that this public demanded based on the tyrannical 'regulating' by RECA. I would lose this market niche.

According to RECA regulations, all licensed members must hold security deposit and rental income "in trust" and report these figures every year to RECA. My business model was thriving because it attracted residential investors that did not want anyone "holding" their rental income. These clients wanted to receive their rent money directly from their tenants' vs waiting for funds to clear through a 3rd party. The clients did not want that needless administrative control. I did not see the value in the needless paperwork either. My business model was transparent, protected my clients from fraud and didn't require regulating.

I had no desire to sell real estate or manage rental income and budgets as licensed property managers do nor did I want to be involved with commercial management and waste my life in board meetings.

I was not going to work from a broker office. My priority was to be in a home office to be a present mother.

I chose to be an independent contractor to avoid this political red tape, power tripping bullshit. I went into business to make money for myself not to make money for the list of brokerage and advertising fees and membership dues and continuous learning costs, etc…or to be under the thumb, or the foot, of an arbitrary corporate bully.

Why should I have to give away thousands of dollars and my limited time to take courses that do not pertain to my business activities just to be governed and audited and always indebted by fees to an independent council I did not get any benefit from? I had every reason to believe that they would always keep a poker in my fire. My lawyer advised that they would have to serve me with a court order to enforce anything upon me so, I would await a court order.

I had built this business literally with my own blood, sweat, and tears and it took me 10 years to grow it and I did it without any resources from the real estate industry. For 10 years I had not needed access to anything that being an industry member would provide. I did not need access to MLS and all the forms and resources I used were provided by the Edmonton Apartment Association (now Alberta Residential Landlord Association). The Landlord and Tenant Advisory Board and the Residential Tenancy Dispute and Resolution Services were the only other support organizations I ever needed assistance from. According to the Residential Tenancies Act, I was acting completely within the law as an appointed landlord agent.

The following two page inserts were printed from Service Alberta's website www.servicealberta.gov.ab.ca/pdf/rta/definitions.pdf

Both pages are very clear that I had a right to act on behalf of residential owners as a landlord agent and those owners had a right to authorize me.

DEFINITIONS

There are a number of words that are commonly used in the RTA, regulations, and in the rental business. Understanding what these words mean, and how they are used, is an important part of understanding what residential tenancies are all about.

These are plain language definitions for the commonly used terms in this guide.

A

Abandon	An action of a tenant who leaves the residential premises before the end of the tenancy, without giving notice to the landlord that they are leaving.
Abandoned Goods	Any property a tenant leaves behind after they move out of the residential premises.
Abatement Of Rent	A reduction in the amount of rent a tenant is required to pay to the landlord. An abatement of rent can occur on a one-time-only basis; for a specified period of time; or be on-going.
Agent	A person who has been given the authority by another person to undertake certain activities on their behalf. Examples include: • A leasing agent who is given the authority to enter into a residential tenancy agreement with a tenant on behalf of the landlord. • A building caretaker who is given the authority to enter the residential premises to make repairs on behalf of the landlord.
Agreement	See Contract definition
Assign Or Assignment	A person assigns their right or obligation to another person, or the written document that transfers a right or obligation. • An example is the tenant in a fixed term tenancy wants to move out of the residential premises before the end of the residential tenancy agreement. The tenant finds someone else who will move in and take over the tenant's rights and obligations. The tenant wants to assign the residential tenancy agreement to this other person.

www.servicealberta.gov.ab.ca/pdf/RTA/Definitions.pdf

105

Inspection Report	A written report that the landlord and the tenant do together at the beginning and end of the tenancy. The report records the condition of the residential premises before the tenant moves in, and after they move out. The inspection report done at the beginning is often called the move-in inspection report, and the one at the end is often called the move-out inspection report. The residential premises **must** be fit for someone to live in. The RTA says the inspection report has to be in writing; that both the landlord and tenant should be present when it is done; and that both should sign it after it is done. • The RTA says the inspection report **must** include certain statements that **must** be signed within the report. • A landlord can do the inspection without the tenant being present if the landlord has offered the tenant two inspection times and the tenant does **not** agree to attend. • A copy of the move-in and move-out inspection reports **must** be given to the tenant as soon as they are completed.

L

Landlord	The legal owner of the residential premises, or some other person that has control of the residential premises. • A property manager, leasing agent, caretaker, building manager, or any other person who controls whether someone can rent the place is a landlord. • A person who, in law, has the same rights as the landlord is a landlord. Examples include the heirs of the landlord; secured creditors acting on their security; or someone who obtains ownership from the landlord. • Any person who has a right of possession of the residential premises and the right to go to court to ask for enforcement of the landlord's rights is also a landlord. An example of this is a tenant who has entered into an agreement with the landlord to assume the role of landlord in renting out units within specified residential premises.

11

If companies like ComFree, Uber, and Airbnb can exist competitively how can there be any justification in denying my unique competitive business model?

CHAPTER 19
Pay Poor Liberty Tax of 17,000

My upper back and shoulders were in so much pain that I went for four chiropractic treatments over the next couple weeks to try and alleviate the pain. Massage and heat treatments were not helping. The chiropractic treatments did not release all the pain either. It was still always there, reminding me of this monkey on my back that I could not shake off.

Upon updating my bookkeeping I noticed on my spreadsheets that my "new revenue" income for the months of January to April was already $17, 000 lower than the income in that same time period of 2012. That is a significant difference in income and I attributed that decrease to the lack of my website and advertising presence and fear of accepting any of the new clients that were being referred to me.

This drop in income caused a great deal of anxiety as I worried about how much worse this was going to get. I had just become accustomed to dreaming big and now my big dreams were turning into a nightmare.

While sipping my coffee on Saturday morning and reading the St. Albert Gazette I came across a classified ad for a Property Manager to handle both residential and commercial properties that stated a real estate license was NOT required. I had come across other ads on line as well that indicated a real estate license was not required. Why was RECA not "cracking down" on ads and industry members like this instead of focusing so hard on my business?

Before finishing my coffee I had removed the freeze off of my Vistaprint website www.slysolutions.ca. I refrained from activating my advertising on www.rentfaster.ca to prove that I was being fair in not competing directly with their industry members. I figured as long as I remained low key behind the scenes that RECA would not have reason to believe I was as much of a threat to their industry members. I still did not believe that was fair though. Property owners should have the choice to hire out an agent who did not control their rental income and at that point I had been the only one advertising that service.

How can RECA have jurisdiction to deny the public that right? I could not let them. Wasn't there competition laws in Canada?

Facebook weather forecast:
We are expecting 2 to 3 feet of drama this evening with a chance of bullsh!t blowing in from all directions!

CHAPTER 20
Take a Ride on the BS Railroad

The dreaded email follow ups from Tricia Hickey started coming on May 14, 2013. I have just copied our email correspondence as factual proof and will share my thoughts on it after you've read it...

From: Tricia Hickey
Sent: Tuesday, May 14, 2013 11:06 AM
To: sylvia@slysolutions.ca
Subject: File 003228 - Request for contact

Hello Ms. Germain,

On April 26, 2013 you were sent a letter outlining that you were trading in real estate and required a licence with RECA in order to continue as a property manager. I would like to know if you have ceased the activities that constitute a trade in real estate. Please contact myself as soon as possible so that we may clear up this matter.

Please contact me directly at 403-685-7942. I can also be reached toll free at 1-888-425-2754.

Thank- you,

Tricia Hickey

Professional Conduct Review Officer
Audits & Investigations
Real Estate Council of Alberta (RECA)

From: Sly Solutions [mailto:sylvia@slysolutions.ca]
Sent: May-15-13 12:59 PM
To: Tricia Hickey
Subject: Re: File 003228 - Request for contact

Brian ████████ at Miller Thomson is quite familiar with regulatory law and has reviewed the cease and desist letter dated April 26, 2013 and does not agree that I am trading in real estate. He believes, as do I, that the sections of the Real Estate Act referenced trace back to the act and inclusion of 'sales and purchases' and that the scope of what defines property management in the act is so broad that any landlord could be deemed as 'trading in real estate'.

My lawyer also shares my belief that my business activities reflect more closely those of an on-site manager with more than one site and should be considered exempt from licensing requirements. I have already been an independent contractor for 10+ years in the private sector without any valid complaint registered against me with the BBB or with RECA and have not proven to pose a threat to the real estate industry. I hold copies of job listings found on line for property managers not requiring a real estate license including one in the April 27, 2013 issue of the St. Albert Gazette. In light of this I will not be disrupting service to my existing clients and expect that you will reconsider my business activities as exempt from your licensing requirements.

Thank you,
Sylvia Germain

2013-05-22   10:35 AM

Hello Sylvia,

Thank you for your response. I believe the section your lawyer is referring to is Section 2(1)(a) of the Regulations pursuant to the *Real Estate Act*. This section reads as follows:

Exemption from Act

2(1)   The following persons are exempt from the Act as it relates to acting as a real estate broker, except Part 2, Division 2:

(a)   an on-site manager who, on behalf of a real estate broker or an owner of residential property,

(i) maintains residential property,

(ii) collects rent on behalf of the broker or owner in respect of residential property,

(iii) shows residential property to prospective tenants, or

(iv) receives applications in respect of residential property from prospective tenants,

but who does not negotiate or approve leases or rental agreements or hold rental or other money in respect of residential property on behalf of the broker or owner;

To qualify as an on-site manager your primary residence must be within the residential property. (Please refer to the Information Bulletin titled "Trading in Real Estate as a Real Estate Broker" enclosed for further clarification or click on the following link: http://www.reca.ca/consumers/content/legislation-bulletins/information-bulletins/trading-in-real-estate-as-broker.html). Since you do not live on-site, this exemption does not apply to you. Regardless of the on-site exemption, you are advertising on behalf of your clients, which is not a listed exemption from the Act. The activity of advertising is considered a trade under section 1(x)(iii) of the *Act* which states the following:

(x)   "trade" includes any of the following:

(iii)   an offering, advertisement, listing or showing of real estate for purchase or sale;

Sale is further defined in section 1(w.01) as the following:

(w.01)   "sale", in respect of real estate, includes an exchange, an option, a lease or any other disposition of an interest in real estate;

Advertising properties on behalf of clients for the purpose of leasing those properties requires a licence. You have been advised since May 14, 2013 that you are to cease these activities immediately. I will follow up with you on Friday May 24, 2013 to confirm your decision. At that point a determination will be made on the appropriate response to your failure to cease activities requiring a licence.

If you have any questions please feel free to contact me directly at 403-685-7942.

Thank you,

Tricia Hickey
Professional Conduct Review Officer
Real Estate Council of Alberta (RECA)

Okay, so the argument at this point as to why I need to cease and desist a $100,000+ per year business service that is obviously in great demand, is because I do not live on these sites and I know how to write and post an ad on-line. Wow! Does anybody reading this see any reasonable logic to this? How are those two points posing any risk, either singly or doubly, to my clients or their industry members? How does a broker license, that takes 3-5 years on average to attain, make me more apt to coordinate repairs and answer tenant calls any better? How does a broker license polish my marketing skills in writing up and posting effective rental ads on Kijiji and other rental websites? It just does not. Why is this even an argument?! Did these girls really not have anything better to do?

Well, obviously not because one week later, on May 28, 2013 my lawyer calls me to share that Tricia Hickey contacted him to explain why the "on-site" manager exemption was not applicable in my case. Thank goodness my lawyer had done more of his homework and approached a different loophole angle with her. I was directly employed by my clients and that was yet another reason to exempt me from broker licensing as per their exemption allowances. Tricia played the 'colour' versus 'color' game and claimed that RECA perceived "direct employee" to mean that my clients would have to withhold income tax from their payments to me but said she would check with her "boss" to see if this loophole would suffice to consider me exempt.

Seriously? What kind of high school game was this? Again, what the hell did it matter whether I paid income tax through each individual client or I paid taxes on my whole income directly to Revenue Canada myself? How does this hold any weight on the activities I'm performing any more than the argument of whether I reside on or off the premises?

And, it stated in their Real Estate Act that RECA officers were not even entitled to contact legal counsel acting on an industry member's behalf.

This was so ludicrous it was making me scream out loud. I was no longer fearful, I was fucking angry. I was no longer understanding of the point of this regulatory body. They were not regulating or looking at evidence. I was being railroaded.

I started googling these RECA conduct review officers and found quite a few posts related to Tricia Hickey slandering other people. Really now? These were all young power hungry wolves I was up against. I was going to have to find a bigger dog than me to fight them off.

I thought there was no point in filing a complaint with their executive director, Bob Myroniuk, because this whole fiasco was quoted to have been initiated by information received by the executive director as of August 2, 2012.

I called Alberta Human Rights Commission to get their assistance on who I should file my complaint with. When I explained my story of RECA threatening administrative penalties and cease and desist orders to me as an independent contractor, the commissioner I was speaking with was in disbelief. He even admitted himself that he knows of other people who do exactly what I do for landlords. They just did not advertise it I guess. He explained that RECA was not in their jurisdiction to regulate and that I would have to file a complaint with Service Alberta who was the governing body for RECA. **He did also advise me that RECA did not have any legal rights to administer an "administrative penalty" against me if I was not already governed by them as an industry member.** This commissioner empathized with my situation and suggested I simply tell RECA to "fuck off and then sue them for harassment, lost income, and court costs". That is exactly what I intended to do.

CHAPTER 21
Backstabbing Lies

I ignored Tricia Hickey's voicemail on June 5, 2013 inquiring if I have ceased all unauthorized activities.

On June 10, 2013 Tricia Hickey emails me again inquiring if I have ceased trading in real estate without a license.

2013-06-10   10:24 AM

Hello Ms. Germain,

I left you a message on June 5, 2013 regarding you trading without a license and I am following up to inquire whether or not you have ceased trading in real estate without a license. Can you please advise whether or not you have ceased?

If you have any questions please feel free to contact me directly at 403-685-7942.

Thanks,

Tricia Hickey
Professional Conduct Review Officer
Audits & Investigations
Real Estate Council of Alberta (RECA)

On June 13, 2013 Tricia Hickey emails me again threatening fines and summarizing a long winded play by play trail of her harassing telephone calls and emails to me. She includes reference to her contacting my lawyer on May 27, 2013 to dissuade him from supporting my stand and claims here that "my lawyer now concurs that I do require a license to continue operating my business". I call bullshit!

2013-06-13   1:49 PM

Hello Ms. Germain,

On April 26, 2013 you received a letter explaining that your activities as a property manager require a license and that you must cease your unauthorized activities. On May 22, 2013 I received an email from yourself explaining that you are not going to cease your activities and that you were advised by your lawyer, Brian ███████, that you do not require a license. On May 27, 2013 I spoke with your lawyer and explained why you require authorization. After he reviewed the legislation, he is now concurs that you do require a license in order to continue operating your business. On June 5, 2013 I left a voicemail message for yourself inquiring if you have ceased your unauthorized activities. On June 10, 2013, after receiving no response from yourself, an e-mail was sent to yourself inquiring if you have ceased your activities. To date, I have not had any form of communication with yourself since your e-mail on May 22, 2013 explaining you were not going to cease your activities.

An inquiry into the education department shows you have not made an attempt to contact our education department to begin the process of becoming licensed.

Kindly contact me by **June 20, 2013** to advise whether or not you have ceased your unauthorized activities. If I do not receive a response by yourself by **June 20, 2013** an administration penalty will be issued to yourself for trading in real estate while unauthorized. A reminder that failure to cease your unauthorized activities can result in fines of up to $25,000 per occurrence.

If you have any questions please do not hesitate to contact me directly at 403-685-7942.

Sincerely,

Tricia Hickey
Professional Conduct Review Officer
Audits & Investigations
Real Estate Council of Alberta (RECA)

My lawyer had called me on May 28, 2013 to inform me that Tricia contacted him and they discussed the "direct employee" loophole that she was supposed to inquire about with her boss and we were waiting to hear back on that. He did not "concur that I required a license to continue operating my business". What lawyer does that to a client he is assisting? I already had plenty of reference to believe that Brian ████████ was the honest one here. It was bad enough that she went behind my back to dissuade my lawyer but to blatantly lie to me was inconceivable.

And, like hell if was I going to "kindly" contact her by June 20, 2013.

She could issue whatever administrative penalty she wanted to. I was not going to pay it.

Tricia Hickey's ears must have been ringing louder than the fireworks that Canada Day because on July 2, 2013. Just as I was getting defense assistance from my Service Alberta friend I received her next coercing email.

From: Tricia Hickey
Sent: Tuesday, July 02, 2013 4:12 PM
To: sylvia@slysolutions.ca
Subject: File 003228

Hello Ms. Germain,

I sent you the email below on June 13, 2013:

> On April 26, 2013 you received a letter explaining that your activities as a property manager require a license and that you must cease your unauthorized activities. On May 22, 2013 I received an email from yourself explaining that you are not going to cease your activities and that you were advised by your lawyer, Brian ████████, that you do not require a license. On May 27, 2013 I spoke with your lawyer and explained why you require authorization. After he reviewed the legislation, he is now concurs that you do require a license in order to continue operating your business. On June 5, 2013 I left a voicemail message for yourself inquiring if you have ceased your unauthorized activities. On June 10, 2013, after receiving no response from yourself, an e-mail was sent to yourself inquiring if you have ceased your activities. To date, I have not had any form of communication with yourself since your e-mail on May 22, 2013 explaining you were not going to cease your activities.

An inquiry into the education department shows you have not made an attempt to contact our education department to begin the process of becoming licensed.

> Kindly contact me by **June 20, 2013** to advise whether or not you have ceased your unauthorized activities. If I do not receive a response by yourself by **June 20, 2013** an administration penalty will be issued to yourself for trading in real estate while unauthorized. A reminder that failure to cease your unauthorized activities can result in fines of up to $25,000 per occurrence.

If you have any questions please do not hesitate to contact me directly at 403-685-7942.

On June 13, 2013 I received a phone call from your lawyer who explained that you are currently working on becoming an employee of the owners, thus exempting you from requiring a license. On June 18, 2013 I left a message for your lawyer as well as today. Since the June 13, 2013 phone message I have not had any update on your progress or what alterations you have made to your business in order to comply with the Real Estate Act.

Kindly contact me by **July 5, 2013** to advise whether or not you have ceased your unauthorized activities. If I do not receive a response by yourself by **July 5, 2013** an administration penalty will be issued to yourself for trading in real estate while unauthorized. A reminder that failure to cease your unauthorized activities can result in fines of up to $25,000 per occurrence.

If you have any questions please do not hesitate to contact me directly at 403-685-7942.

Tricia Hickey
Professional Conduct Review Officer
Audits & Investigations
Real Estate Council of Alberta (RECA)

Note that she had given a deadline of June 20, 2013 to contact her in her June 13, 2013 email and in this July 2, 2013 email she claims having called my lawyer on June 18, 2013. Why was she calling my lawyer again, incurring legal costs to me, and why was she calling two days before the deadline June 20, 2013? I should have had two more days yet before she harassed anybody.

Tricia imposes a new three day deadline now of July 5, 2013 to advise her that I've ceased my business. I pondered whether I should just send her an email saying I had ceased business activities to test if she would get off my case but I did not trust that she would accept that without further interrogation.

CHAPTER 22

On-Site Manager Exemption Request

After 6 full months of this unreasonable harassment, my RECA story had become the topic of conversation with all of my family and friends, clients, and everyone else I met. My circle was always amazed that RECA was still focusing on me and my business when I had not done anything wrong and was providing a very valuable service.

On that Canada Day weekend, while at a house warming pig roast dinner party for my best friends, I met another very close friend of theirs. We were enjoying a shot of whiskey and a cigar (Yes, I would smoke the odd cigar while on vacation celebrating life or under severe pressure) and I began sharing my RECA story after he asked me what I did for a living. Well, low and behold, it turned out he worked with Service Alberta Audit and Investigations. Holy shit! Jackpot. What were the chances that I would meet the other BIG dog I needed to chase these wolves away.

He questioned me more on my business procedures and, in his opinion, believed that RECA's case against me was not strong enough to carry out a cease and desist order and agreed that this council sounded like they were on a personal mission. A mission that could have already escalated beyond his ability to have a golf course chat with anyone about it to easily put a halt to it.

Unfortunately, he was not familiar with any of the female names I dropped, not even executive director, Bob Myroniuk. I was not familiar with any of the male names he mentioned either.

Regardless of him not being familiar with these gals, I was invited to forward some of the pertinent emails and letters I had received from RECA and he assisted me with the following letter of response directly to executive director, Bob Myroniuk asking again to be considered for exemption under real estate exemption regulation 111/96. Hallelujah! There was a God.

I had my lawyer review my response letter, who responded with "Great letter" and I mailed it out July 3, 2013 to the attention of Bob Myroniuk. I was not able to get an email address for him. Go figure. I probably would not give out my email publicly if I was in his position either. I was pretty turned off from the email shit I was getting myself these last six months and dreaded my computer notification sound every time a new email came in. My heart would race and a frustration would set in before I even checked to see who it was from in fear that it was RECA, again.

I decided to advise Tricia by email on the morning of July 4, 2013 that I had sought assistance from Service Alberta Audit & Investigations and had mailed a response letter to them as of July 3, 2013. Seven minutes later she replied with a very simple "Great. Thank you."

From: Sly Solutions [mailto:sylvia@slysolutions.ca]
Sent: July-04-13 10:05 AM
To: Tricia Hickey
Cc: Brian ████████
Subject: Re: File 003228

Please be advised that with the assistance from a member in the Audit and Investigations Branch of Service Alberta, I have forwarded a letter of response to RECA in the mail as of July 3, 2013.

Sylvia Germain,

SLY SOLUTIONS LTD

Right Tenants, Right Price, Right Time!

Real Estate Council of Alberta
Suite 350, 4954 Richard Road SW
Calgary, Alberta
T3E 6L1

July 3, 2013

Attn: Bob Myroniuk

Dear Sir,

Further to your letter of April 26th 2013, and subsequent correspondence with your office, I wish to be considered for an exemption under the Real Estate Exemption Regulation 111/96.

Specifically, I operate my business consistent with 2 (1) (a) of the Exemption Regulation:

On behalf of an owner of a residential property my role is to:

(i) maintain residential property
(ii) collect rent on behalf of the owner
(iii) show property to residential tenants, or
(iv) receive applications in respect of residential property from perspective tenants
but does not negotiate or approve leases or rental agreements or hold rental or other money in respect of residential property on behalf of the owner.

All rents and security deposits are handled by owners. The role that I perform for my owners is consistent with that of an on-site manager. The regulation does not define an on-site manager and my contention is that RECA's interpretation "whose primary residence is within the residential property" is not binding in law. It is the duties I perform that are important under the Act not where my primary residence is located.

With regards to the concerns you have raised under Section 17 and specific reference to sections:

1 x (iii): I do not show Real Estate for purchase or sell.
1 x (v) I do not hold myself out as trading in real estate
And with regards to advertising, my owners pay all bills for advertising and only my contact name is provided consistent with the exemption to show properties or receive applications.

In closing, I respect the role of the Real Estate Council of Alberta but my business is consistent with the exemption regulation.

Warm Regards,
SLY SOLUTIONS LTD
Per:

Sylvia Germain.

CHAPTER 23
Stress Leave -Take a Ride on Jet Planes & High Speed Trains

The next day I was on a plane to Europe with my best friend for a 3 week itinerary to hike the Swiss and French Alps, eat and drink wine in Italy, and sail Croatia. I had booked the trip, extremely last minute, only three weeks before when my best friends, Tom and Lynda, encouraged me to take a sanity break from this living nightmare I was caught up in. They were going for six weeks, I would go for three weeks.

I always was a last minute travel bug and always wanted to go to Europe. It was a lot of money to spend on myself but I had worked damned hard for that money and it was better spent on me than on filling RECA's coffers.

"Stress leave" was what had been advised by the Naturopath I consulted with in June trying to get a handle on my insomnia and fatigue, and weight gain and changed menstrual cycle. I had gained 8 lbs since January and had always weighed a very regular 117 lbs for many years only fluctuating by maybe 3 - 5 lbs. The Naturopath specialized in bioidentical hormones and thought I was still young to be experiencing perimenopause or menopause at 43 and explained that ongoing stress can bring on hormonal disruptions. He did a full hormonal screen on me that did not raise any alarming imbalances but prescribed a bare minimum thyroid medication to appease me. He also prescribed prometrium progesterone to help me sleep as I was against taking sleeping pills.

I paid $350 for this one hour consultation that was not covered by my health insurance plan. It was a ridiculous amount of money to pay but I had probably spent over $500 already on health food store sleeping aids, stress reduction pills and every weight loss pill showcased on Dr. Oz.

I pulled from my previous experience as a Personal Fitness Trainer trying every exercise program I had used in the past to achieve weight loss and some new ones. No amount of brisk walking, elliptical, planks, squats, or weight training, kickboxing or Zumba was budging a pound off and I had coupled all this exercise with the 80/20 clean eating rule.

The other advice from the Naturopath was to "remove the stressors". I did not have a nice cushy job with employee benefits that allowed my any kind of disability leave. That is one of the drawbacks of being self-employed. I did however continue to get paid residual income no matter where I was in the world so, vacation stress leave was the only thing left I could do for myself. I was thinking I should be able to lose a few pounds hiking the Alps for a whole week!

It was not easy trying to coordinate child care for my 13 year old daughter for a three week period at the last minute. Not taking a getaway break would probably have broken me so I HAD to run away from this stress and I managed to juggle her Father, my Mother, and my daughter's best friend's Mom. Knowing she was in great hands made it a little easier to be gone three whole weeks.

My subcontractor, Moe, was more than willing to be on call 24/7 for my clients and tenants and I set my email auto reply and telephone answering machine to let every caller know that I was on stress leave hiatus in Europe and would be back July 28, 2013.

Tom headed to Croatia alone the first week to spend alone time with his family and Lynda and I headed to Chamonix, France to climb Mont-Blanc with transfers to the Italian side of the Alps. I was not anywhere nearly as conditioned as Lynda for this strenuous hike as she is a marathon runner but I did it. Every day for 5-6 hours. It was very exhilarating and empowering and exactly what I needed to start my stress leave with to burn off the anxious energy that had imprisoned me since January 2013. I still never lost a pound though.

Glacier caves at Montenvres Mer De Glace were definitely a sight to see with 400 steps to go down, and 400 steps back up. Paragliding off the mountain in Chamonix, France was the biggest adrenalin rush. I recommend it to anyone who is adventurous but still fears jumping out of an airplane. After stops in Germany and Switzerland, Lynda flew to Croatia to join Tom while I spent the second week touring by myself in Italy.

I took in all the pasta, wine, sights, scenery, trains and shopping that Italy had to offer in Tuscany, Florence, Siena and Milan. I think I understand now why the pizza and pasta does not cause obesity in Europe... because they have so many hills to walk up and down. Everywhere! I still did not lose a pound though. I was in the most beautiful basilicas in the world, at the right time, and believed that my prayers for peace in my life would have to be heard here.

At one point, on one of the tours, I came across another mother and her daughter who was about the same age as my daughter. The mother did not have a wedding ring and I assumed they were travelling alone together. It made me miss my daughter so much and I sat crying on the steps of the Divina Belleza Duomo in Siena wishing I could share this experience with my daughter as well. I felt so alone, empty and shattered in that moment, like an orphan child. So, this is what running away feels like. Yet as bad as I felt at that moment, I had no desire to be back in the thick of dealing with threatening and demanding entities constantly tugging at me.

The third week, I flew to meet Lynda for a week of sailing in Croatia. This was definitely an adventure. Remember, I booked this trip at the drop of a hat without researching anything because Lynda already had it figured out. I had been envisioning beautiful yachts and butlers serving me wine and hors d'oeuvres and sunbathing in pillowy lounge chairs. Ha! Joke was on me.

There were 8 of us on this trip from all over the world. Lynda and I in the 40-55 age range and the other 6 aged 21-25. Interesting. The skipper, under 30 as well, met us for orientation at the marina café and instructed that we first had to shop for groceries, as a group, for food that would last all of us a few days. Say what? We had to cook this food ourselves too? Wow! I had already earned my Girl Guide badges a long time ago. This is not what I thought I signed up for. But, it was what it was and so be it.

It was a pretty funny sight to see me struggling with all my oversized luggage going down the dock of the marina while everyone else just had a backpack. We stopped in front of the smallest sailboat in the marina. No. You're kidding, right? How were we going to fit 8 people plus a skipper plus my luggage in there? The skipper gave Lynda and I the 'honeymoon suite' as my luggage would not fit anywhere else. I had to sleep with my legs over top my suitcase at the foot of the bed. Sweet!

The toilet did not actually flush without being manually pumped but we had a land stop every day to save us with showers and flushing toilets, and restaurants. Hallelujah! Ahoy mates and mateys!

I would love to elaborate on each place I visited as that would be more fun to write about however this is not a travel blog. I am including some of these travel stories though because I think both my readers and myself need a change of pace.

Travelling European airports, train stations and with taxis by myself was very frustrating and was enough to make me wonder if I still had a "kick me" sign on the back of my head.

I departed from my friend in Switzerland and headed to Florence, Italy on the high speed train which went very smoothly. The taxis were lined up there for the picking but obviously not for me. I don't even remember how many of those taxi drivers I went through showing the address for the bed and breakfast I needed to get to in Tuscany and getting a deer in the head lights look. It was somewhere in the second row of cars I finally found a friendly driver who spoke English and said he would be glad to take me there. It would take 1 hour he said and $100 US. Great!

We enjoyed good light conversation and I was having the taxi ride of my life enjoying the city sights of Florenzia getting tips from him of where and where not to go. The countryside creeped up with its beautiful rolling hills of sporadically dense assorted greenery and I had finally started to relax taking it all in when the car abruptly turned off on a side road in a secluded heavily treed area. The car came to a rolling stop on the side of the road and my relaxed state suddenly turned into a panicked one. I looked at the driver and blurted out "You're not going to kill me, are you?"

He chuckled and explained that the car broke down and he had to call another car in to take me the rest of the way. Oh man, it didn't make sense that another driver would find us on this out of the way dirt road but what did I know. I bummed a cigarette from him thinking I might as well enjoy one last thing before I die and we waited in the 35 degree heat, without air conditioning, for another car.

A car did roll up from the opposite direction and a young couple came out to ask my driver for directions as they were lost. The driver attempted to put the address in his GPS but could not find it. OMG, this had horror movie scene written all over it! The couple were making their way back to their car as my brain and my gut fought over whether I should jump in with them and before I could make a life-saving decision, another taxi rolled up behind us. Whew!

During my amazing stay in Tuscany I experienced trains breaking down leaving us sitting on the middle of a track that we could not walk out of if we wanted to, again in sweaty temperatures without air conditioning. Many taxis had broken down air conditioning as well.

When leaving Tuscany I transferred to Milan on the more reliable high speed train but when I arrived at the Milan train station I got more of the same run around that I was trying to escape. I had booked a hotel within walking distance of the train station, for good reason, and do you think anybody would point me in the right direction for me to get to this hotel. Not. I went to all 4 corners of that very big train station asking taxi drivers where I could find this hotel and each one of them sent me on a wild goose chase. There I was, all alone pulling my awkward oversized luggage and crippled over with my heavy back pack, exhausting myself running in circles being ostracized by taxi drivers who refused to help anyone that would not line their pockets. None of them would even offer to drive me because it wasn't a big enough fare for them to leave their line- up. I was in the middle of a world conspiracy against me.

Finally, a rare, good Samaritan noticed me crumpled and teary eyed in my heap of luggage and pointed me in one of the directions I had already been to and gave me a detailed description of what to look for and what street to cross. Thank-you!

I had scheduled my taxi to pick me up at 4:00 am from my hotel in Milan, Italy the following morning to get me to the airport early enough to allow for expected struggles along the way with language barriers, traffic, or in figuring out the airport. The taxi driver drove up in a slick shiny black mobster car looking perfect for the part in a James Bond movie.

There was no small talk during the ride though and I attributed that to the fact that he was focusing on his high speed driving that had me imagining I was on another high speed train. The estimated 30 minute drive took 15 minutes and the check-in wickets were not even open yet. I was left with nothing to do but hurry up and wait and line up for one last cappuccino. By the time I got my cappuccino the check-in was lined up. I made it through the line-up and was told my luggage was overweight and I needed to pay extra. I was expecting that and handed her my credit card to pay the charge. Oh, but I was not allowed to pay her. I had to go to a different line up across the airport to pay this extra fee and bring her back a proof of payment ticket. Say what?

Off I went, luggage in tow, in pursuit of this separate fee payment wicket with another long line. I got through that line to be told that they could not accept credit card. Huh?! This was Milan, a world shopping haven. How could they not be accepting credit cards in their airport?! I spent the last of my Italian currency at the coffee kiosk. Now I had to find a bank machine.

I eventually made it through the overweight luggage red tape and was starting to worry about missing my flight as I had not even made it through security yet and I always get pulled aside at security. There were no x-ray machines to put our carry- on baggage through just a little Italian man who was randomly choosing who to check and of course, I was chosen.

He pulled me aside and went back to waving others through. He was not speaking English and left me standing there wondering what the heck I was waiting for. I had to go poke him to remind him I was still there fearing I would miss my flight. He motioned to my back pack and then to my tiny little 5" spaghetti strap cross shoulder purse and put up his finger to show "one" only. He was demanding I put that little shoulder purse into my back pack. WTF?! Are you kidding me? He was waving through people who were carrying camera bags plus carry-on baggage but my little 5" purse that sat on my hip only big enough to hold my phone and passport and cash was a problem. It was even smaller than a fanny pack!

They say what doesn't kill you makes you stronger and at this point I should be able to bench press an airplane!

My back pack was literally bursting at every zipper and I envisioned everything popping out like a jack-in-the-box if I dared unzip any of them. I had to unpack my little black purse and pull out a little jacket to wear and stuff my pockets and take out silk scarves and stack them around my neck to make room to repack and stuff my little 5" purse into my back pack. Unbelievable.

By the time I got back home on July 28, 2013, I did not want to be anywhere else. Until 2 days later...

CHAPTER 24
Serv-It Processes

I was back home from Europe just in time to jump hard back into work with month end move-outs and move-ins, cleaning, banking, and getting new sign in documents and move out refund paperwork to clients on top of three weeks of email catch up.

I could not believe that I had not received a single email from Tricia Hickey while I was away. The call history on my home office phone showed that someone from RECA tried calling though so they would have heard on my answering machine that I was in Europe until July 28, 2013 and did not even bother leaving a message this time. I wondered if Bob Myroniuk had received my exemption request letter that I mailed July 3, 2013. I was expecting a response to that request.

Well, I was not even home for two full days when I came home from a long day of tenant moves to find the following "serv-it" notice on my front door.

SERV-IT PROCESS SERVICES

ATTENTION: _Sylvia Germain_

Re: DELIVERY OF COURT DOCUMENTS
To make arrangements for service, please contact: ████████████

TOM WALKER

(780) 424-4868 office/cell 780-504-4570
Office hours: 8:30 AM - 4:30 PM (Mon-Fri)

NO LATER THAN 12:00 (noon) on: _July 31, 2013_

FAILURE to do so will result in a Court Order authorizing us to post the documents to your door. The extra cost of obtaining this Order are quite significant ($500 to $1000). The Court enforces payment of these costs and it is **YOUR FULL RESPONSIBILITY TO PAY!** It would be in your best interest to contact us.

Ok, so I do not know how many people would actually pick up the phone to call this service to make it easy to have court documents served to themselves but I certainly was not one of those people. Not that day. First off, July 31 is a busy day in the life of a landlord agent and I had better things to do on that day than waste my time making it easy for this document server, Tom Walker, to not have to put in much effort for the job he was getting paid to do.

Second, I have had to serve court hearing documents to tenants enough times to know how this process was to be legally and ethically performed. I always was expected to make three personal attempts at serving documents at three different times of the day and sign an affidavit noting the dates and times I tried serving. If those three attempts did not get the documents in their hands I was then able to serve them through registered mail.

I was not calling Tom Walker. He would have to follow the correct process to serve me anything.

The whole month of August 2013 was not as busy for me with new clients, given that I was still not able to advertise, but I stayed busy enough with tenant lease renewals and showings for properties that tenants had given vacating notices for in July.

I had not received any phone calls or emails from RECA regarding my letter to Bob Myroniuk or regarding court documents and I had not found anything posted on my door in that month of August. I was starting to wonder if executive director, Bob Myroniuk had finally reviewed my exemption request letter and decided to leave me alone without notifying me in writing. It really was just the calm before the storm…

There were a few times I heard my doorbell ring as early as 7:00 am and as late as after 10:00 pm. I cannot determine who it was but if it was Tom Walker of Serv-it Processes he was certainly outside appropriate business hours of 8:00 am – 8:00 pm. Even his own office hours stated *8:30 am – 4:30 pm (Mon-Fri)* on his notice form. This was pure harassment.

"Injustice anywhere is a threat to justice everywhere."
-Martin Luther King Jr.

CHAPTER 25
Stalking - RCMP Intervention

On September 4, 2013, as I was in the middle of painting a condo unit in South West Edmonton, my daughter called me in a panic about somebody who kept ringing our doorbell and knocking hard on our front door. She had been trained at a young age to never answer the door. I never knew when a disgruntled tenant might show up on my doorstep and I never answered my door for unannounced visitors. I always had "no soliciting' signs posted on my mailbox as well.

I instructed her to stay calm and to go upstairs and look out her bedroom window to see if there was a vehicle in our driveway or on the street by our house. There was not. The doorbell ringing and door knocking had stopped so I suspected whoever it was had left. I stayed on the phone with her while she went back downstairs to check if something was posted on our door or left in our mailbox. Nothing there. All was ok. It might have been a neighbour. I assured her I would be home as soon as possible but I was at least a 45 minute drive away in rush hour traffic and still had to pack up my painting gear.

It was not even two minutes later that she called me again crying and I could hear the 'ding dong, ding dong, ding dong' and then 'knock, knock, knock, knock' and then again, 'ding dong, ding dong, ding dong, ding dong' and 'knock, knock, knock, knock' with a fierceness that would scare the crap out of any adult, including me. What the fuck?! I tried to remain calm and asked her to go back upstairs and look out her bedroom window again to see if she noticed any unusual vehicles near our house or across the street. She did notice a black SUV across the street that was not typically there so I told her to try and calm herself and to go play outside in the back yard with the new foster puppy we just brought into our home in August while I called the RCMP.

The RCMP station was just down the hill from us so I trusted they would get there within 5 minutes. I promptly reported the suspicious vehicle and harassing stalking behaviour at my personal residence and how scared my daughter was and was assured they would be right there.

I called my daughter back to assure her the RCMP would be there shortly and she claimed the door bell ringing and door knocking had not stopped. Are you kidding me?! I explained she would have to answer the door for the RCMP to answer a couple questions and that they would clearly identify themselves so she knew who was at the door.

I was sick to my stomach and I could not even imagine how my daughter was feeling being all alone in this situation. I had every reason to believe this was RECA and my whole body was vibrating with anger. My drive home was a blur and must have been done on auto pilot as my mind raced with worry.

I made it home to find my daughter on the kitchen floor holding our foster dog and crying. She shared that there were two RCMP officers that came to the house and handed me the business card with their names handwritten on it with a file #2013-1141267. One was female and one was male and the female RCMP officer explained that there was a lady who just wanted to talk to her mom and gave her another business card (copied here) from Dian Kuhtey of RECA with a handwritten note on it to call her.

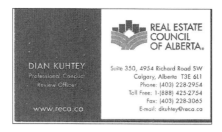

Seriously?! No important documents or life threatening reason to be stalking and terrorizing my young daughter at my personal residence?! This Dian Kuhtey had obviously watched my daughter step out the front door to check the mailbox after her first round of harassing doorbell ringing. Did she really think my 85 lb soaking wet daughter was me?! What kind of human being terrorizes a child, and a puppy, like this for over one hour?

This woman obviously lacked both a heart and a conscience. Obviously that was the prerequisite to be employed with RECA. How many bitches were they going to involve in this Charlie's Angels take down?

My foster rescue puppy, Poppy, learned on that day as well that the doorbell is a BAD thing. We ended up adopting him and to this day, three years later, I cannot train him to calm down when the doorbell rings. The second 'failed foster' rescue dog we adopted, Bella, has picked up on Poppy's anxiety and has unfortunately learned to also attack at every doorbell ring or knock. My daughter and I suffer with anxiety as well from this and everyone in my circle knows to text or call me before showing up at my home and allow themselves in without knocking or ringing the doorbell.

After that unprofessional harassing demonstration from Dian Kuhtey I was not about to show an ounce of respect to her or anyone else in that self-regulated crime unit.

The very next morning I ordered a security camera and filed a follow up harassment complaint with the RCMP. I spoke directly with Constable Joevanazzo about filing harassment charges against RECA. She suggested that she speak directly with someone at RECA first to "warn them off" and so she could get familiar with this regulatory council.

By the end of the day I was advised that Constable Joevanazzo's discussion with RECA resulted in her being told that they were a "government agency" and therefore they had the right to go to any measure to serve me documents. Say what?! The government has a right to fear mongering with children?! Why would I be proud to be Canadian then? An even more infuriating part of this was that they were not a "government agency"! A simple google search of RECA (copied below) showed in the very 1st line descriptor "*Independent, non-government agency responsible for the regulation of the real estate industry…*" It does not read 'Government agency responsible for the regulation of the residential tenancies industry'. It reads "independent *non-government…*" Further research on the Service Alberta website (copied on next page) also reads "*RECA is an independent, non-government agency responsible for regulating real estate, mortgage brokers, and real estate appraisal professionals under the Real Estate Act of Alberta…*"

They lied to the RCMP and the RCMP were accepting it. Wow.

1/18/2017   reca - Google Search

Real Estate Council of Alberta
https://www.reca.ca/ ▾
Independent, non-government agency responsible for the regulation of the real estate industry. Contains consumber information, industry regulations and …

Industry Professionals
real estate appraisal professionals. …
the business of industry …

Consumers
Alberta real estate board consumer …
The Real Estate …

Licensing and Renewals
Licensing and Renewals. The Real
Estate Council of Alberta …

Real Estate Council of Alberta
Real Estate - Eligibility - Licensing
and Renewals - …

Contact
Contact the Real Estate Council of
Alberta. Real Estate Council of …

Eligibility
Eligibility. To become a licensed real
estate, property …

More results from reca.ca »

Service Alberta

MOBILE HOME SITE RENTING

Consumer Contact Centre
780-427-4088 in Edmonton or
Toll-free in Alberta at 1-877-427-4088

Resource:
• *Renting a Mobile Home Site*

Modular Housing Association Prairie Provinces (MHAPP)
The Modular Housing Association Prairie Provinces represents all aspects of the modular housing industry.
780-429-1798
www.mhaprairies.ca/home.aspx

REAL ESTATE

Alberta Real Estate Association (AREA)
AREA is a non-profit provincial industry organization that represents the interests and concerns of 11 regional real estate boards and more than 10,000 REALTOR® member associates and brokers.
1-800-661-0231
www.areahub.ca

Alberta Real Estate Foundation (AREF)
The Alberta Real Estate Foundation funds initiatives related to education and research, housing affordability, land stewardship and environment and industry leadership to benefit the industry and people of Alberta.
403-228-4786
Toll-free in Alberta 1-800-520-2485
www.aref.ab.ca

Real Estate Council of Alberta (RECA)
RECA is an independent, non-government agency, responsible for regulating real estate, mortgage brokers, and real estate appraisal professionals under the *Real Estate Act* of Alberta.
Calgary: 403-228-2954
Toll-free in Alberta: 1-888-425-2754
www.reca.ab.ca

SENIORS

Seniors
Alberta Supports Contact Centre
Edmonton Area: 780-644-9992
Toll-free in Alberta: 1-877-644-9992
www.seniors.alberta.ca

Deaf & Hard of Hearing Society
Deaf or hearing impaired with TDD/TTY units.
In Alberta:
Toll Free TTY/Voice: 1-877-711-3447
Toll Free Fax: 1-877-818-3447
Telus VRS: 403-002-0013
Text Messaging: (587) 989-3447 (local number)

Oak-Net - Older Adult Knowledge Network
Provides information on how Canadian law protects and affects older adults.
www.oaknet.ca

TELECOMMUNICATIONS

Canadian Radio-television and Telecommunications Commission (CRTC)
The CRTC is an independent public organization that regulates and supervises the Canadian broadcasting and telecommunications systems.
Toll-free: 1-877-249-CRTC (2782)
www.crtc.gc.ca/eng/home-accueil.htm

Commissioner for Complaints for Telecommunications Services (CCTS)
CCTS is an independent organization dedicated to working with consumers and telecommunications service provider to resolve complaints relating to telecommunications services.
Toll-free: 1-888-221-1687
www.ccts-cprst.ca

11

On September 6, 2013 a voicemail was left on my home office machine by Dian Kuhtey demanding that I call her before noon to arrange the serving of documents. Had she not heard of registered mail?! And again, why was there now a fourth RECA officer involved? Was Tricia Hickey tired? I know I sure was.

I needed to get more advice from elsewhere again and after more googling I called Alberta Ombudsman. The Alberta Ombudsman supposedly responded to complaints of unfair treatment by provincial government authorities and designated professional organizations. I spoke with Melissa and explained my story. She was shocked at the extent of this harassment by RECA considering how many investors we all know that hire people that provide the same service to landlords. She was sympathetic to the fact that Alberta Ombudsman unfortunately did not have any power or jurisdiction over RECA and referred me to Service Alberta and wished me luck.

Before starting the time consuming work of printing and photocopying my paper trail proof for a Service Alberta complaint I sent an email to Dian Kuhtey and Tricia Hickey, cc'ing my lawyer Brian ████████. I did not have email addresses for Sherry Hillas or Robin Baron.

September 6, 2013

A Police report has been filed (#2013-1141267) in St. Albert on Wednesday, September 4, 2013 in regards to the stalking harassment endured by my 13 yr old daughter by a Dian Kuhtey of RECA at my personal residence. I had to call RCMP after distraught telephone calls from my daughter about someone repeatedly ringing the doorbell and banging on the door without any evidence of a parcel being delivered. Based on the time of the calls from my daughter to the time RCMP showed up to investigate it's calculated that this harassment lasted approximately 1 ½ hrs. This was terrorizing not only for my daughter but for the rescue dog we have just started fostering. We have endured unexplained doorbell rings at all hours of the night and very early morning that are outside of legally acceptable hours for serving documents. **Stay away from my personal residence. If there are communications to present to me please do so in a more professional and legal manner as I would be expected to. Send me your documents by registered mail.**

These repeated interrogations and harassments by 4 different RECA officers without any actual receipt of court documents as of yet has crossed the line of harassment vs investigation for public concern. It demonstrates bullying abuse of power with a color vs colour game play around the true purpose of the Real Estate Act and appears to be a set up to simply line your own pockets. I am aware that RECA has allowed other non-industry landlord agents do provide the same service I do and it's interesting to note that these non-industry agents service lower income portfolios than I do. Hmmm....

RECA website states that they need to provide information on what the complaint is and who filed the complaint. RECA's refusal to divulge this information has me believing that I am a victim of coercion and extortion instigated by Libertas

Property Management who has shown an unrelenting determination to purchase my high end portfolio since August 2012. Carolyn Hackett of Libertas shared with me that she was familiar with Moe ██████, who she recognized on my website, explaining Libertas had recently bought out a portfolio from the Realty Executives brokerage that Moe is licensed with. After unsuccessful attempts by Carolyn to buy out my portfolio, Moe ██████ coincidently underwent RECA investigation regarding his business affiliation with Sly Solutions Ltd and our business procedures. That investigation was settled with a simple administrative order to ensure that his brokerage of record was clearly noted on my website. Moe was not ordered to cease business activity with me or advised that our business activities were illegal. Hmmm...

Carolyn Hackett's documented persistence in following up on my position in selling my portfolio has also been coincidently paralleled with RECA's increasing harassing pressure on me. How coincidental it also is that once I questioned Tricia Hickey on the involvement of Libertas in this interest to investigate my business Libertas completely stopped trying to negotiate with me.

I am NOT operating a brokerage. I am NOT earning income from real estate sales or purchases. I do not advertise anything on MLS or utilize any services or benefits geared for your industry members. I have not misrepresented myself to anyone as being a licensed realtor or property manager. I do not hold security deposits or rent in my accounts or trust accounts and have not misappropriated anyone's funds. I have not proven to pose a threat to the public or the real estate industry outside of being successful competition for the industry members you govern. RECA does not hold record of proof that I have acted beyond the scope of an on-site manager.

I will not be bullied into ceasing business activities that have been my live-lihood for 11 years already without your governing guidance nor will I allow myself to be coerced into sharing my honest hard earned income through your licensing requests or into handing over my rental portfolio to Libertas Property Management.

RECA's website also states that they act with a level of reason. The involvement of 4 different RECA officers threatening me with phone messages to cease and desist or face a $25,000 is not reasonable nor is communicating with my legal counsel behind my back to discourage him from supporting my defence. Stalking my personal residence and terrorizing my family definitely is not reasonable in my eyes or the law's eyes.

I have been advised by an Alberta Human Rights Commission Officer to literally tell you to "F&#* off" and that RECA has no legal right to fine me any admin-istrative penalty if I am not an industry member. I believe RECA also does not have the right to deny the general public from employing or hiring whoever they want for whatever purpose they are willing to pay for. Bullying me into licensing denies my clients the service they seek from me. These clients don't want their money held in trust by a licensed Property Manager! **I am filing a complaint with Service Alberta Audit and Investigations and I am prepared to sue/countersue RECA for undue excessive harassment causing hardship, coercion, attempted extortion, and my projected loss of income during the months I refrained from contracting new business which also resulted in physician documented stress related illness plus all the legal costs incurred. I will also bring this story to the media.**

Service Alberta would be my next hoop...

> *"Dear life, I have a complete grasp on the fact that you are not fair.*
> *Please stop teaching me that lesson."*
> **-Anonymous**

CHAPTER 26
Service Alberta Run Around

On September 13, 2013 I marched into Service Alberta with my complaint file and first sat down with Meghan McKeeman who read my chronological order of events and listened to my whole story with the appropriate jaw dropping dismay. After exhausting myself with reliving this whole story, again, she claimed she was unable to help me as this was a matter of "business against business" versus a consumer issue and Service Alberta was for consumer complaints. Are you fucking kidding me?!!!! I cannot remember but I must have broken into tears because she expressed deep apologies and then provided information on FOIP to offer some kind of resource to help me in proving who filed the August 2, 2012 complaint with RECA and what the complaint was. This FOIP information ended up being another dead end street, of course.

She then sent me to Audit & Investigations which is where I thought I should have been considering this was a complaint against the conduct of a regulatory body that Service Alberta supposedly governed. Keep in mind I had already received assistance from someone in this office who wanted to remain anonymous, of course.

When I got to the Audit & Investigations office I was let in to one of the offices and the lady (I cannot remember her name) who I began to reiterate my spiel to, stopped me right away and explained I needed to do this with the Consumer Investigations Services department. That's where I just came from and by this time I felt like I was on Candid Camera.

I did not even bother getting her card and just made my way back to the consumer complaints department biting my tongue all the way. This second time around I was sitting across from Martin Roy who I handed my complaint file to for him to quickly review and began explaining my case again. He showed absolute disinterest and was extremely condescending towards me with comments such as "well if RECA believes you're doing something wrong, you must be." Excuse me? Obviously he was also golf buddies with these corporate bullies.

I asked to speak with someone in command in that office whom he claimed was 'Kelly Refah' and that she was away for the week. Of course she was. I demanded that he pass my complaint file on to Kelly Refah and asked for a business card with her name (and his) and contact number for me to follow up with her.

I have no doubt that he put my complaint right into the file 13 garbage.

*"If you make the choice to serve the public,
Then serve the public, Not yourself."*
-Anonymous

CHAPTER 27
The $5000 Administrative Penalty

On September 20, 2013 I received the registered mail envelope from RECA that enclosed a Notice of Administrative Penalty dated July 9, 2013 (while I was in Europe). So, this was the document that my family was being so unconscionably stalked and harassed for?! I was expecting an actual court document.

The condensed version states that they expected me to pay $5000 to them within 30 days or pay them $1000 to dispute it in front of their own hearing panel. That sounded more like a money sting than anything.

I had already been disputing it and clearly defending my position since January 2013 to four of their officers AND their executive director already so why would I pay them $1000 to explain myself again?!

My lawyer advised me that paying the $5000 would not guarantee that they would get off my back as there was nothing stopping them from claiming there was another complaint against me and reopening another case. That would eventually be proven. This was not a court order. I am not licensed through them and I was not lining RECA's pockets without a court order.

REAL ESTATE
COUNCIL
OF ALBERTA.

Our Ref: 003228
Your Ref:
Please ask for: Tricia Hickey
Direct Dial: 403-685-7942
e-mail: thickey@reca.ca

Private and Confidential

Sly Solutions Ltd.
Sylvia Germain

July 9, 2013

Dear Ms. Germain:

NOTICE OF ADMINISTRATIVE PENALTY

Enclosed herewith please find a Notice of Administrative Penalty in regard to your contravention of section 17 of the *Real Estate Act* (Act) as described therein. Full particulars are set out in the Notice.

In accordance with section 83.1 of the Act, you have 30 days as of the date of service of the Administrative Penalty to appeal the Administrative Penalty. Should you choose to appeal, you must provide written notice of appeal describing the penalty being appealed and reasons for the appeal, along with security of costs of the appeal in an amount that is the lesser of 3 times the Administrative Penalty being appealed or $1,000.00. The written notice of appeal and security for costs of the appeal must be provided, preferably together, but in any event both must be supplied within the 30 day appeal period. Otherwise, your appeal will be statute barred.

A copy of section 83.1 of the Act is enclosed for your information. Should you choose not to appeal, payment of the Administrative Penalty must be made no later than 14 days after the appeal period has expired. Please be aware that a failure to pay the amount set out in the notice may result in the commencement of legal action against you pursuant to section 83(3) of the Act for the amounts owing in respect of the notice and costs.

Suite 350, 4954 Richard Road SW, Calgary, AB T3E 6L1 Telephone: (403) 228-2954 Fax: (403) 228-3065
Toll Free: 1-888-425-2754 Web site: www.reca.ca E-mail: info@reca.ca

Should you have any questions, please contact Tricia Hickey, Professional Conduct Review Officer, at 403-685-7942.

Thank you for your attention to this matter.

Yours truly,

Bob Myroniuk
Executive Director

Part 6 - General
Section 83.1 - Appeal of Administrative Penalty

83.1(1) A person to whom a notice to pay an administrative penalty is given under section 83(1) may, within 30 days after receipt of the notice, by notice of appeal in writing to the executive director, appeal the decision to a Hearing Panel.

(2)   A notice of appeal under subsection (1)

    (a) must

        (i) describe the administrative penalty appealed from, and

        (ii) state the reason for the appeal,

    and

    (b) must be accompanied with security for costs in an amount that is the lesser of 3 times the administrative penalty imposed and $1000.

(3)   On receipt of a notice of appeal and security for costs, the executive director shall refer the matter to a Hearing Panel, which shall hold a hearing.

(4)   Sections 41 and 42, but not sections 43 to 47, apply to the hearing of an appeal under this section.

(5)   The Hearing Panel on an appeal may

    (a) quash, vary or confirm the administrative penalty, and

    (b) make an award as to costs of the investigation that resulted in the administrative penalty and of the appeal in an amount determined in accordance with the bylaws.

(6)   The Hearing Panel's decision under this section is final.

(7)   The executive director shall serve a copy of the Hearing Panel's decision on the appellant.

2007 c39 s47

Our Ref: 003228

REAL ESTATE COUNCIL OF ALBERTA

NOTICE OF ADMINISTRATIVE PENALTY

To: Sly Solutions Ltd.
Sylvia Germain
▮▮▮▮▮▮▮▮▮▮▮▮▮
▮▮▮▮▮▮▮▮▮▮▮▮▮▮

In accordance with section 83 and the Bylaws of the *Real Estate Act* RSA 2000 c R-5, (Act), the Executive Director of the Real Estate Council of Alberta (RECA) is of the opinion that Sylvia Germain (Ms. Germain) and Sly Solutions Ltd., have jointly and severally contravened section 17 of the Act and hereby assesses an Administrative Penalty jointly and severally against them in the amount of **$5,000**. The evidence giving rise to the Executive Director's decision is as follows:

On behalf of an owner of a residential property, you advertise and show properties to potential tenants. These activities constitute trading in real estate and require authorization and a license with RECA.

You argue that you fall under the exemption of an "on-site manager". You, and your legal counsel, have been instructed that to meet this exemption you must reside on the residential property. As you do not reside on the property in question, this exemption does not apply.

The Executive Director is of the opinion that the above noted conduct is in violation of section 17(a) of the Act which sets out that:

17 No person shall

> *(a) trade in real estate as a real estate broker,*
>
> *(b) deal as a mortgage broker,*
>
> *(c) act as a real estate appraiser, or*
>
> *(d) advertise himself or herself as, or in any way hold himself or herself out as, a mortgage broker, real estate broker or real estate appraiser*
>
> *unless that person holds the appropriate authorization for that purpose issued by the Council.*

In accordance with section 83 of the Act and Part 4 of the Bylaws, the Executive Director hereby assesses an Administrative Penalty in the amount of **$5,000** against Sylvia Germain and Sly Solutions Ltd. jointly and severally.

The circumstances of this matter indicate the following aggravating and mitigating factors were considered:

Aggravating Factors

1. You were warned numerous times, both verbally and written, by a Professional Conduct Review Officer from RECA, that your activities required a license.

2. You refuse to accept the fact you require a license and continue to trade without authorization.

Payment of this Administrative Penalty shall be accepted by the Executive Director as complete satisfaction of the amount of the penalty and no further proceedings under Part 6 of the Act will be taken against Sylvia Germain and Sly Solutions Ltd. in respect of the contravention. A person who pays an Administrative Penalty may not be charged under the Act with an offence in respect of those contraventions.

This sum of **$5,000** is payable to RECA within thirty (30) days of the date of issuance of this Notice of Administrative Penalty. If Sylvia Germain and Sly Solutions Ltd. fail to pay the amount set out in this notice, the Executive Director may commence legal action against Sylvia Germain and Sly Solutions Ltd. to recover the amount owing in respect of the Administrative Penalty as a debt due to RECA.

If Sylvia Germain and Sly Solutions Ltd. disputes this Notice of Administrative Penalty in accordance with section 83.1 of the Act, Sylvia Germain and Sly Solutions Ltd. may appeal it to a Hearing Panel. Sylvia Germain and Sly Solutions Ltd. will be given a full opportunity consistent with procedural fairness and natural justice to present evidence before the Hearing Panel and make representations in relation to the contravention.

If Sylvia Germain and Sly Solutions Ltd. have any questions in regard to this Notice of Administrative Penalty, please contact Tricia Hickey, Professional Conduct Review Officer, at RECA.

DATED this ___/0___ day of July, 2013.

REAL ESTATE COUNCIL OF ALBERTA

Per: _____

Bob Myroniuk
Executive Director

CHAPTER 28
Education/Experience
Exemption Request

October 3, 2013 another email rolls in from Tricia Hickey. I had not heard from her since July 4, 2013 when she acknowledged I had mailed a letter to them.

This following inserted email states RECA received another complaint about my company. Yet, AGAIN, it is not divulged as to who filed it and what it was regarding as per the natural laws of justice. I do not believe there was a complaint and if there was, it was probably from Carolyn Hackett of Libertas Property Management, again.

I found it really odd as well that in the last paragraph of the email, she comes across with a much warmer approach than ever in trying to understand my hesitation in becoming licensed and adds that I might want to inquire about education exemptions with the education department. Really? After nine months of harassing me and demanding money from me and being aware of my educational and mortgage lending background, she is just now suggesting the possibility of an education exemption! Maybe this should have been offered to me before slamming the guilty verdict and administrative penalty on me.

My last email to her and Dian Kuhtey must have hit a nerve for her to be acting with more professionalism. I still felt like I was being led on a dead end wild goose chase.

From: Tricia Hickey
Sent: Thursday, October 03, 2013 11:09 AM
To: sylvia@slysolutions.ca
Subject: File 003853

Hello Ms. Germain,

The Real Estate Council of Alberta (RECA) has received another complaint on your company, Sly Solutions Ltd. RECA has previously communicated, both verbally and in writing, that your activities require authorization under the *Real Estate Act*. Unfortunately you have refused to cease activities that require a license and as a result you were issued an Administrative Penalty on September 20, 2013. As of October 3, 2013, your website is still offering services that require authorization. These services include advertising properties on behalf of owners and showing properties on behalf of owners.

It is mandatory that if you want to continue to offer the same services to your clients that you become authorized to trade in real estate through RECA. In the meantime you are required to immediately cease your activities that require authorization to trade in real estate in the Province of Alberta. As we recognize you have a right to appeal the Administrative Penalty until October 20, 2013, we will not proceed with further action until that time. RECA strongly encourages you to cease all activities requiring a licence, or a stronger sanction may be deemed appropriate.

You have stated you have been doing property management for many years and this company is your livelihood that you have worked hard to build and maintain. Part of your hesitation for becoming a licensed real estate associate may have to do with the length of time it will take to complete your education in order to obtain your license. Please be aware that the Executive Director has the authority to grant exemptions regarding education when appropriate. You may want to inquire with the education department to see if you qualify for any of these exemptions. The education department can be reached at 403-228-4954, toll free at 1-888-425-2754, or by email at education@reca.ca.

If you have any questions please do not hesitate to contact me directly at 403-685-7942 or toll free at 1-888-425-2754.

Thank you, **Tricia Hickey**

I figured I had to turn over every stone I could before I would ever see the end of this bullshit so I exhausted myself again writing another letter to executive director, Bob Myroniuk and the education department. I wanted to speak directly to Bob Myroniuk but could not get past an administrative secretary. She did provide me an email address though. Hopefully she would not intercept and redirect my email to junk mail. I sent that education exemption request (copied on next page) along with a supporting resume on October 7, 2013.

I cc'd my lawyer as well as the RCMP constable that I filed my harassment/stalking complaint with.

SLY SOLUTIONS LTD
Right Tenants, Right Price, Right Time!

Real Estate Council of Alberta

October 4, 2013

Attn: Bob Myroniuk; education@reca.ca

Further to email correspondence from Tricia Hickey of October 3, 2013, and subsequent correspondence with other RECA officers since February 2013, I wish to be considered for an education exemption. I did mail a letter to the attention of Bob Myroniuk on July 3, 2013 requesting consideration for exemption under the Real Estate Exemption Regulation 111/96 as an on-site manager and that request was never specifically acknowledged before receiving notice of an administrative penalty on September 20, 2013 (but dated on July 9, 2013).

My request for an education exemption is based on:
- Over 25 years of professional experience and education in managing financial applications and character assessment as per my attached resume.
- 10+ years already providing landlord services as a 'self-regulated' independent contractor in the private sector for residential investors.
- 13 years experience in the financial industry including personal lending, mortgage lending, investment advising, personal financial planning, accounting, and marketing.
- Small Business course completed at U of A as well as a Government training program for small business completed through Anderson Career Training Institute in 2009
- My business practice is consistent with the on site manager exemption regulation

My marketing and lending skills have been the basis of my success in assisting residential owners with finding the right tenants. Many inquiring owners do prefer to deal with licensed managers however the clients who do hire me are more concerned with the skills I bring, the experience I have, the trust I earn, and the ability to control their own rental income.

I have no interest in pursuing the areas of commercial or rural real estate or in residential sale transactions or in operating a brokerage, all of which seem to be the largest focus of RECA's REAP educational requirement. This information will not help me in finding tenants.

Your acknowledgement of this request and consideration of my professional background with 10+ years already providing this landlord service coupled with consideration for my clients' choice is appreciated.

Warm Regards,
SLY SOLUTIONS LTD
Per:
Sylvia Germain,

Enclosures: Personal Resume

That same day I managed to reach Kelly Refah of Service Alberta by phone. I was not surprised to hear that she had not received my complaint file. Go figure. I felt like I was in a bad espionage movie with the whole world conspiring against me.

She, like everyone else at Service Alberta, also did not want to hear about my complaint and waved me off with "RECA knows their business better than her and if they concur I need a license, so be it". Wow. Worst dream ever. I was trying to file a complaint based on the lack of professionalism and harassment by this regulatory body and their refusal to divulge what I had a right to know! I was not trying to get her to decide whether I should be licensed or not. I knew I was banging my head against another brick wall and I prayed that something would give with the education exemption request.

I had been literally on my knees praying for a miracle break through or a rich man to come and save me but I received this negative email response the very next day, October 8, 2013, from the education department:

From: education inbox
Sent: Tuesday, October 08, 2013 12:09 PM
To: sylvia@slysolutions.ca
Subject: RE: Education Exemption Request

Hello Sylvia,

As Property Management falls under the "umbrella" or Real Estate the following would be required for you to be exempt from any of the education requirements regarding being licensed as a property manager.

Examples: Applicants who may have satisfactory knowledge and/or experience include:

A. Real Estate (Property Management)

i)   Real estate industry professionals (i.e. associates, associate brokers, brokers) who have been authorized by RECA and practiced in Alberta continuously for more than 10 years and who have been out of the industry for less than 4 years.

ii) Lawyers whose area of practice related to real estate and who have more than 5 years of experience continuously practicing real estate law in Alberta within the last 6 years.

iii) Former staff of RECA, AREA, Alberta real estate boards, BOMA or IREM who have 5 years of experience dealing with real estate practice issues in Alberta within the last 6 years. Also, former staff of other Canadian real estate regulators with 5 years of experience dealing with real estate practice issues within the last 6 years.

iv) Real estate property managers who traded in real estate in Alberta continuously for more than 5 years within the last 6 years and where their authorization will be restricted to property management.

Unfortunately, as you have never been authorized by RECA you do not meet these requirements. Nor do you qualify for the exemption from the Act which you mentioned below. I have also included other information regarding exemptions below.

Exemption from Act

2(1) The following persons are exempt from the Act as it relates to acting as a real estate broker, except Part 2, Division 2:

(a) an on-site manager who, on behalf of a real estate broker or an owner of residential property,

(i) maintains residential property,

(ii) collects rent on behalf of the broker or owner in respect of residential property,

(iii) shows residential property to prospective tenants, or

(iv) receives applications in respect of residential property from prospective tenants,

but who does not negotiate or approve leases or rental agreements or hold rental or other money in respect of residential property on behalf of the broker or owner;

(b) a person who is licensed under the Retail Home Sales Business Licensing Regulation (AR 197/99) and is carrying on business in accordance with that Regulation;

(c) a non-profit organization, or an employee, official or member of the organization, with respect to its or his

(i) leasing or renting of subsidized residential premises,

(ii) collecting or offering or attempting to collect money payable as

(A) rent for the use of subsidized residential premises, or

(B) contributions for the control, management or administration of subsidized residential premises,
or

(iii) acting, advertising, conducting or negotiating directly or indirectly in furtherance of any activity referred to in subclauses (i) and (ii) on behalf of the owner or other person in charge of the subsidized residential premises.

To become licensed as a property manager in Alberta you will have to become eligible to enroll in the program. Please see http://www.reca.ca/industry/content/licensing-renewals/real-eligibility.html for further information.

The Property Management Program consists of two courses – the Fundamentals of Real Estate and Introduction to a Career in Property Management. *Once these courses have been completed and you have gotten a certified criminal record check (only good for 6 months so don't get this until you are almost ready to become licensed) you will have to join a brokerage that practices property management.*

Melody Wry
Education Administrator
Real Estate Council of Alberta (RECA)
Suite 350, 4954 Richard Road SW, Calgary, AB T3E 6L1
Office: 403-228-2954 Toll-Free: 1 (888) 425-2754 Fax: 403-228-3065
www.reca.ca

Note on the first page under *Examples: Applicants who may have satisfactory knowledge and/or experience include:*

(iv) Real estate property managers who traded in real estate in Alberta continuously for more than 5 years within the last 6 years and where their authorization will be restricted to property management.

This is exactly what I already proved to be and requesting exemption as! Are these people not reading my words? I had 10+ years of continuous landlord agent/property manager experience in Alberta plus I had a business background in credit, lending, and marketing PLUS real estate investment training with the reputable Real Estate Investment Network. For people who were accustomed to being just as wordy as I with longwinded emails and letters I would think they would have the capability to read other people's words. Nobody was reading my words or even pretending to consider my defense.

The very last paragraph informs me that I need to start with taking *2 courses – the Fundamentals of Real Estate and Introduction to a Career in Property Management* and then I *will have to join a brokerage that practices property management.*

As if I'm going to cease operating my own successful landlord agent business to go make money for some broker providing their textbook service that my clients DO NOT WANT! It is ludicrous.

These people were so blinded by their self-regulatory power they could not even realize common sense. Or…it was their usual strategy to break people with mind games until they were destroyed. Like police detectives. But they are not police.

"Dear Santa, all I want for Christmas is my own island where I won't have to deal with mean people."
-Anonymous

CHAPTER 29
Happy Holiday Wrappings

I received an early Christmas slap in the face from my lawyer when I opened the $2500 invoice for legal services in 2013. Ouch! It just was not fair to be being billed when these monkeys were still all over my back. I felt like I was the one doing all the work in researching the Real Estate Act, letter writing and complaint filing and looking for other resources to help. My jaw fell to the floor when I realized that his standard fee was $5850 before he had discounted me $3350.00. Holy crap! I thought he charged $500 per hour not per phone call! At least he considered the discount for all the incoming calls from RECA that I should not be held accountable for. I did have to be understanding of the fact that he did not know the monkeys were still on my back.

Even though I had not received monthly billings from him I had entered a contract with him so I promptly paid his $2500 but was determined to get that money back somehow from RECA through some form of legal action.

RECA was not alone in perpetrating this extortion game, Carolyn Hackett of Libertas Property Management was holding the lighter that lit the flame under me.

On December 31, 2013, Carolyn Hackett found it appropriate to poke me with another email hoping I was ready to sell. Happy New Year to me! Her year-end numbers must have been looking a little bleaker than mine and I chose to wait until the holiday season was over before giving her any thought.

From: Carolyn Hackett
Sent: Tuesday, December 31, 2013 11:07 AM
To: sylvia@slysolutions.ca
Subject: Opportunity

HI Sylvia- hope all is well and you are enjoying the holiday season. As another year approaches I thought I would write to you again to see if you are interested in getting rid of your portfolio. As per previous communications, you were considering at one point in getting out of the business. Please do let me know if you are interested in selling at this time or in near future. Thanks in advance.

Happy New Year!

Regards,

Carolyn Hackett
Owner
REALTOR

Why did these real estate gals always poke me during a holiday long weekend? Canada Day, Labour Day, now New Year's Eve. Is that what they're taught in the extortion module of their conduct review officer training? Is it part of their real estate broker training?

It does not take a rocket scientist to determine that Carolyn Hackett was the other complaint that Tricia Hickey eluded to in her October 3, 2013 email to me. This is more than coincidence. Again.

Rather than ignore Carolyn's inquiry I chose to play it cool in letting her know that the challenges that I had been up against were not enough to break me. Because I still had such a lucrative gig she would have to present me with an enticing offer for me to consider negotiations. I might have considered a negotiation at this point if she would have thrown me a number.

From: Sly Solutions [mailto:sylvia@slysolutions.ca]
Sent: January-10-14 9:17 AM
To: Carolyn Hackett
Subject: Re: Opportunity

Hi Carolyn, this business does present ongoing challenges that make me question how long I will continue. However, I have built a lucrative residual income and would need to be presented with some kind of offer before considering negotiations with anyone. Feel free to throw a number my way for me to consider...

Sylvia Germain

2014-01-10   11:41 AM

Hi there- thanks for your reply. We would have to know your revenue you numbers on a monthly basis before speaking about price.

Regards,

Carolyn Hackett
Landlord Liaison
REALTOR

She would not throw me a bone back with any offers and wanted to know my monthly numbers first. She had already determined my numbers back in August 2012 and I assume she was aware of reason to believe those numbers would have dropped significantly. I did not offer her anymore leverage.

"Starting tomorrow, whatever life throws at me,
I'm ducking so it hits someone else."
-Anonymous

CHAPTER 30
Happy New Girl! Again!

A new gal from RECA, Melissa Savidant, Administrator, Panel and General Counsel emailed me on January 27, 2014 demanding payment of the $5000 administrative penalty that they issued on me on July 9, 2013.

Oh my God. How many more women, from how many different departments, were they going to sick on me? And why were they using email communication for such matters? It seemed rather unprofessional to me.

And why were they not poking me in November or December to pay this administrative penalty that they claimed was due in October 2013? Did RECA have that many administrative penalties issued to be so behind in collecting? Or did Carolyn Hackett follow up again on her whining to RECA because I was still not showing interest in negotiating with her?

I would wait for the legal action that Melissa Savidant threatened me with versus succumbing to their illegal action and I ignored her email.

Dear Ms. Germain,

As outlined in the Notice of Administrative Penalty dated July 10, 2013, the amount of the Administrative Penalty was payable within thirty (30) days. The time within which you were required to pay has now elapsed and you have failed to pay the Administrative Penalty in the amount of $5000.

The Administrative Penalty must be paid by no later than 7 days from the date of this letter. If you fail to pay the amount of the Administrative Penalty, the Executive Director may commence legal action against you to recover the amount owing as a debt due to the Real Estate Council of Alberta.

You must contact me immediately at the address indicated below.

Melissa Savidant
Administrator, Panels and General Counsel

Of course I did not want to waste any more of my time, money and already very limited energy in a legal tangle in a court room but after a whole year of this harassment it was obvious that a courtroom would be inevitable.

On April 7, 2014 Melissa opted to professionally forward another payment demand notice by registered mail. Oh my God. Just serve me the damn court order already so I could countersue. This game was wearing me out! My common sense told me that if RECA really believed they were in their right they would have served me a court order by now.

I wanted to speak directly to executive director, Bob Myroniuk and I thought that maybe he would take my call this time seeing as they were chasing me for money. I called the office on April 10, 2014 and was patched to his assistant Cheryl Badgley. Bob Myroniuk would absolutely not take any direct calls. Wonderful. Of course he would not take direct calls. I learned not to take calls either since this fiasco started in January 2013. I would always let it go to voicemail.

It was not fair that I could not speak directly to the name that was noted on these notice letters as the sender. It was not his signature on these letters. The signature started with a 'C' and appeared to be Cheryl Badgley's signature. How could I be sure that Bob Myroniuk was even behind this Charlie's Angels ambush? What if all these power tripping gals were working behind his back to get me? Speaking with Cheryl Badgley would be a complete waste of time.

I was not communicating with my lawyer anymore since getting invoiced for $2500 as it did not make any sense to incur more legal costs until I was ready to be defended in a court room. My mind and shoulders were constantly weighed with how I would be able to afford to go up against these bullies in a court room. What if I dished out $25,000 from my home equity in legal costs and these bullies were still able to stomp me down? I could not trust in anything these days.

I could not handle the sleepless nights of over analyzing anymore and finally broke down and went to my doctor for sleeping pills on April 17, 2014. Sleeping pills were completely against my belief system but the natural remedies were not helping. I had to succumb.

> *"When the debate is lost, slander becomes the tool of the loser."*
> **-Socrates**

CHAPTER 31
Better Business Bureau Defamation

I did not have to look at my book keeping spreadsheets to realize that I received zero new business clients in April 2014. When I did compare my previous year's income spreadsheets it was evident that in 2012 I had brought in $16,435 in new business income during January-April. 2013 showed $6,999 for January - April, a significant drop. And, for January – April of 2014 a measly $1,315 in new business income.

This was a serious loss of income and instilled a great fear in me. The business I had worked so hard to build to such success with integrity was crumbling before me. And I had not even done anything wrong. I had no idea what I was going to do.

I knew if I tried advertising my website again it would poke the sleeping bear, Carolyn Hackett, again. I had not heard anything from RECA in a few months now and I did not want to rock the boat yet.

Summer time had come and I was distracting myself with lease renewals and day to day tenant issues. Then, I received a phone call from a potential new client, who had been referred to me by an existing client, who questioned me on the 'F' rating on Better Business Review account. SAY WHAT?! I had an 'A+' rating, not an 'F'. I have never had an 'F' in anything in all of my life! He proceeded to share with me that there was a blurb on my account advising a business alert for Sly Solutions Ltd due to government action by the Real Estate Council of Alberta. Government Action?! As per my Google printout in Chapter 25, **RECA is an independent, non-government agency.**

How in the hell did they have a right to defame my business name online without a legal court decision?! I had not even been contacted by the Better Business Bureau to be able to defend myself and it was in their rule book to do so for any complaint. I've inserted the following screen prints from the BBB website below…

There it was on the first page. The "L" in my luck had been replaced with an "F". The third page showed RECA's slander. All I could do was cry. And drink. I did not have any fight left in me at this time. I was already reaching a breaking point at the time I called Carolyn Hackett about her kijiji ad to purchase portfolios. This was all too much for me to take. After all of the brick walls I had already run into in this nightmare I knew I was only going to hit another one by even confronting Better Business Bureau. That's it. I was done.

BBB BUSINESS REVIEW

What is a BBB Business Review?

THIS BUSINESS IS NOT BBB ACCREDITED

Sly Solutions Ltd

(780) 458-5008

View Additional Phone Numbers
Street Address on File, St. Albert, AB T8N 6H8
http://www.slysolutions.ca

‖ There is an alert for this business ‖

 On a scale of A+ to F
Reason for Rating
BBB Ratings System Overview

Share   Print   0

BBB Business Reviews may not be reproduced for sales or promotional purposes.

BBB Accreditation

Sly Solutions Ltd is not BBB Accredited.

Businesses are under no obligation to seek BBB accreditation, and some businesses are not accredited because they have not sought BBB accreditation.

To be accredited by BBB, a business must apply for accreditation and BBB must determine that the business meets BBB accreditation standards, which include a commitment to make a good faith effort to resolve any consumer complaints. BBB Accredited Businesses must pay a fee for accreditation review/monitoring and for support of BBB services to the public.

Reason for Rating

BBB rating is based on 13 factors. Get the details about the factors considered.

Factors that *lowered* Sly Solutions Ltd's rating include:

Failure to have a required competency license.

Customer Complaints Summary

0 complaints closed with BBB in last 3 years | 0 closed in last 12 months

Complaint Type	Total Closed Complaints
Advertising / Sales Issues	0
Billing / Collection Issues	0
Problems with Product / Service	0
Delivery Issues	0
Guarantee / Warranty Issues	0
Total Closed Complaints	0

Definitions | BBB Complaint Process | File a Complaint

Customer Reviews Summary   Read customer reviews

0 Customer Reviews Customer Reviews on Sly Solutions Ltd

Customer Experience	Total Customer Reviews
Positive Experience	
Neutral Experience	
Negative Experience	
Total Customer Reviews	**0 Customer Reviews**

Read Customer Reviews | Submit a Customer Review | See Trends in Customer Reviews on Sly Solutions Ltd

Government Actions

The following describes a government action that has been resolved by either a settlement or a decision by a court or administrative agency. If the matter is being appealed, it will be noted below.

On July 10, 2013 RECA issued an Administrative Penalty against Sylvia Germain and Sly Solutions Ltd.

In accordance with section 83 and the Bylaws of the Real Estate Act RSA 2000 c R-5, (Act), the Executive Director of the Real Estate Council of Alberta (RECA) is of the opinion that Sylvia Germain (Ms. Germain) and Sly Solutions Ltd., have jointly and severally contravened section 17 of the Act and hereby assesses an Administrative Penalty jointly and severally against them in the amount of $5,000.

On behalf of an owner of a residential property, Sylvia Germain and Sly Solutions Ltd advertised and showed properties to potential tenants. These activities constitute trading in real estate and require authorization and a license with RECA. The required licence and authorization had not been obtained by Ms. Germain.

More information may be obtained by contacting RECA at 1-888-425-2754.

What government actions does BBB report on?

Advertising Review

BBB has nothing to report concerning Sly Solutions Ltd's advertising at this time.

What is BBB Advertising Review?

Additional Information

BBB file opened: 26/05/2011
Business started: 01/01/2010

Type of Entity
Limited

Contact Information
Principal: Sylvia Germain (Owner)

Business Category
Real Estate Rental Service

As an afterward here, I did finally find the energy to inquire with the Better Business Bureau in September 2015 as to why I was not notified by them of this to defend myself. I would have been too beaten down to fight them anyway but I did deserve to have that opportunity. I was forwarded, by email, the original letter that was mailed to me in March, 2014 and I noticed that the address on that letter was incomplete which explained why I did not receive it.

My address is duplicated in St. Albert, one is North, one is South. So, I often get mail for the South address recipient and put it back in the mailbox with 'South' written on it. That person does not do the same with my mail if they receive it.

Part II

FREE Parking

"You can close your eyes to the things you do not want to see, but you cannot close your heart to the things you do not want to feel."
-Johnny Depp

CHAPTER 32
Community Chest– Pay Hospital Much More Than $200

The constant pressure of putting out new fires with tenants and properties all day every day should have been enough to distract me from the worry of what might happen to my business, and me, but I was literally sick about it. There's positive stress from overworking to make money. The stress becomes quite negative when one is overworked and losing money due to defamation out of one's control.

My upper back and shoulders were so tense and in so much pain from the weight of my burdens and the muscle relaxants, hot baths, and heating pads were not helping. I scheduled massages and chiropractic treatments that didn't help and went for reiki treatments to try and release the negative energy. That helped in the moment but the burdens were still always there and so the pain would come right back.

I had also been putting on more weight and my menstrual cycle became unpredictable for the first time in my life. I wondered if I was entering early menopause and began reading every health book and magazine I could find trying to diagnose myself. I had always been a healthy person and proactive with my health which is evident in my business involvement with Melaleuca wellness products and as a certified personal trainer in my earlier years.

All of my blood work appeared normal and doctor's opinions indicated that my body was just suffering from too much stress. Aside from the shingles outbreak I was hit with in February after I was ambushed by Sherry Hillas, I had not been in a doctor's office since February 2010. Three years without needing a doctor. The 3-4 years of mental and physical distress would make up for that and eventually lead to further entanglements with my health insurance company. The constant fear and stress I was under tortured my mind with anguish making me also turn to sleeping pills for the first time in my life. My immune system was compromised causing more frequent infections of various kinds. My thyroid became sluggish and abdominal ultrasounds indicated cysts on my liver. These were all stress related conditions.

The stress burned me right out. I was no longer able to cope rationally. The anger and frustration eventually turned into hopelessness and bitterness challenging my friendships and left me unable to be a positive role model for my daughter.

The financial stress made me feel desperate and I was so fearful of losing my independence through losing my business that it sabotaged intimate relationships.

After falling into depression I went against my belief system and agreed to take anti-depressants.

I had been living as a prisoner in my own home, scared to answer my door for anyone or have the lights on at night or keep the blinds open. My heart would race every time my phone or doorbell rang. Every new email alert had me full of anxiety. I used to welcome these forms of communication because it could have meant new business but there was almost a zero chance of new business coming my way now with that BBB defamation portraying me as a common white collar criminal. I was now constantly on guard for the next attack.

That next attack came from my own body. It was July 2014 and I had been enjoying a fun and relaxing camping weekend with my boyfriend (I explain more about him in Chapter 33) and his sister at the time. It was so good to get away from my prison home where nobody could find me. After a few days of a holiday trailer bed I was looking forward to my own bed though.

My boyfriend and I unpacked the trailer at his home in Sherwood Park and I packed up my two rescue ruff dogs in my truck and set off on the 45 minute drive to my home in St. Albert.

Now that the relaxing was done I started dreading what kind of messages would be waiting for me at home. I had only driven for maybe 5 minutes and started to feel a tightening in my chest that I've never ever felt before. It was a really heavy hollow feeling and I was wondering if this is what heartburn was. I had never experienced heartburn before so I was not sure what that felt like. It had been a couple hours since I had eaten lunch and I had eaten a healthy salad and tuna croissant sandwich, nothing that should cause heartburn.

It was more of a discomfort than a pain and I continued driving while trying to take deep breaths. I had been driving 20 minutes already with the same tightness and just as I veered onto the Anthony Henday freeway I felt the discomfort travel up my chest and up my neck into my jaw and the back of my ears. In turn I was feeling lightheaded and then broke into a cold sweat.

The word "heart attack" came into my head. How could I be having a heart attack? I was a healthy person that ate well and exercised and was only a very casual smoker.

I should have pulled over and called 911 but I did not. I had my cell phone next to me with 91 typed in, ready to hit the last 1…but I had 2 dogs with me and what would happen to them if an ambulance took me away. They would not bring my dogs with me. I also had my daughter waiting for me at home who had just been dropped off by her dad and I needed to get home.

I focused on driving with every ounce of strength and willpower telling myself "I'm going to be ok, I'm going to be ok". I still had at least 20 more minutes of driving.

This feeling was not going away and I kept telling myself "You're almost there" thinking I would drive myself straight to emergency at the Sturgeon Hospital in St. Albert. As I entered St. Albert, I argued that thought with the fact that I still had 2 dogs in my truck and could not just leave them in my truck at the hospital. I would have to drop them off at home and then get to emergency.

I made it home, got the dogs in the house, and as faint as I felt shared with my daughter that I needed to get myself to the hospital because I thought I was suffering from a heart attack. I did not want to cause another scene in my home with an ambulance there. My daughter collapsed into a heap on the floor crying about what was going to happen to me and did not want to be left alone.

Of course she would not want to be left alone. What the heck was I going to do? I sat on the garage step hanging on to the door and tried taking really deep slow breaths and praying for the feeling to go away. It did go away a few minutes later. I should have still gone to emergency to get checked but I still did not want to leave my daughter alone freaking out so I rested until the next morning when I phoned my family doctor.

My doctor did not want to believe I had a heart attack due to actual heart issues. She was under the impression it must have been stress induced anxiety. Common sense told me it did not matter whether we called it a heart attack or an anxiety attack, it was still caused by stress.

I went under a barrage of heart testing and abdominal testing over the next 2 months. Heart testing indicated sinus arrhythmia and brady arrhythmia. The abdominal ultrasound showed I had a cyst on my liver and a gallbladder polyp. The stress was attacking my mind and now my body.

Summer went by and I had not heard another word from RECA since April 2014. I was not hearing from new clients either now that my business name was slandered on Better Business Bureau. A simple google of my personal name or business name brought up the RECA website and the reference that there was an outstanding $5000 administrative penalty against me as well as the BBB 'F' Rating defamation. They had effectively destroyed me.

I was also losing existing clients which is inevitable as owners start choosing to sell. I had lost $2000 per month in residual monthly commissions within the 2 month period of August and September with no hope of replacing with new clients. It was devastating to me and I felt like such a failure all of a sudden when I had to make the decision to drop one of my subcontractors that had been helping with South Edmonton properties.

I tried to see it as a blessing in disguise and that maybe it was the universe's way of telling me I needed to take a break and change my path. I was so burned out already from all the pressures on me in the last couple years that I was unable to spark new creativity. I just could not figure out what new path I could follow. So then I would think that the universe was just testing my strength as a business woman and that I just needed to get over this hurdle and then I would reap the rewards for the pain I endured.

I needed to rest though. Rest my mind and my body. I did not have a support system to be able to do that though. Sure I had family and friends to talk to but I did not have a spouse to lean on or anyone else to help pay the bills. No one to allow me to fall and catch me.

CHAPTER 33
Take a Walk on the Boardwalk

What I did have at that time that I was grateful for was the boyfriend I had been dating for a whole year now. We met through Lifemates, an expensive and elite dating agency that I paid $4000 to join right after coming back from Europe. Funny true story, but I mentioned in Chapter 31 how I prayed for a rich man to save me and 6 weeks later I met a tall, handsome millionaire who made his money in real estate investing in the right place, at the right time. He had a great family and we had a lot in common and after 9 months of dating I could see a real future with him. I was starting to think that the universe really did send him to save me and that just maybe, he would want to marry me.

We had been making future plans and discussing how we would combine our families. He was settled in Sherwood Park, a suburb far North East of Edmonton and at least a 45 minute drive away. I was settled in St. Albert, North West of Edmonton, waiting for my daughter to finish high school before making any big changes. His youngest was already in her graduation year and the next coming year would be ideal for buying a house together.

I felt desperate to have a new address where RECA could no longer find me. I imagined a new found freedom from feeling imprisoned in my home, and worry every time I checked my mailbox. I could understand first hand now why I was taught in business classes to use a post office mailbox for business versus a home address. At the time of receiving those tips though I was a strong believer in that I needed to be as personable as possible to earn the trust of clients with high end properties. A general post office box might appear as though I had reason to hide. I never imagined in a million years that I would be given reason to hide now.

As much as I wanted a new life, being the independent woman I had worked so hard to become had my heart and my mind constantly battling each other. I loved this man and his older children and family and I wanted to be with him. The little voice in the back of my mind was always challenging me with questioning how smart it was to jump into another house with a man who was not marrying me. My house was all I had left. He respected my independence as a business woman but I was losing my business so how much longer would he respect me if I could no longer be independent? Would he have my back if I lost everything I worked for and suffered a mental break down? Or would he be turned off by such desperation? Would he think he could control me if I allowed him to carry me for a while? I had to keep telling myself that he was sent to me for a reason and it had to be for a good reason.

Trusting was my biggest challenge in life. I had not been able to trust anyone or anything for years, especially after the mind games I had been the brunt of for almost 2 years now with RECA. I just tried to be grateful and believe that everything would work out as it should.

I was going to believe that I would get a fairy tale ending with a Prince, a wedding dress, a new home, and a new business venture with my new life mate partner...

CHAPTER 34
Pay Luxury Tax

My fairy tale ending was manifesting even better than I had imagined it. My boyfriend was finally ready to leave Sherwood Park and grace the suburbs of St. Albert and we were designing our dream home. My best friends were building their dream homes in the same neighbourhood (he was the builder) and I was so excited about all the dinner parties and fun we would have, not to mention the fact that RECA would no longer be able to harass my family in my home as they would no longer have my home address.

My boyfriend and I discussed keeping my home as a rental investment to supplement the income I was continuously losing. My portfolio dropped from 60 properties to 30 and could not be replenished while I was being slandered on the RECA and BBB websites. Keeping my home was important to me and would make me feel like I still had some independence. I was so scared of losing my independence and being under someone's thumb and I was grateful to my boyfriend for understanding this.

The deposit was put down on the best lot of the bunch, at the end of the lake, where I envisioned myself sitting on my balcony writing my book series about my rescue dogs. We made a list of everything we all wanted and needed in a house. I put my heart into doodling and drafting ideas that would be appreciated by everyone in our soon to be blended family. The blue prints were drawn up. I was so proud and feeling like I was finally being rewarded for all the seeds I had sown in my life that were now coming up roses.

But every rose has its thorn and tensions started to rise. My boyfriend was beginning to stress about money and I was always stressing in the back of my mind about losing my business and my independence. I was believing that the continuous gradual loss of my income was scaring him as much as it was scaring me. As I mentioned earlier in the book, I never wanted to feel like I was under any man's thumb by not having control of my own life.

My fear manifested itself when I found out that he had retracted his deposit on our dream lot and put his money down on the worst lot of the bunch, backing directly onto the railroad track and a clump of trees. It was a lot that we had both stood on and agreed was a poor choice for some sucker so this was the biggest slap in the face. No discussion about it at all. It showed me the controlling side of him.

If he had discussed his reasons for wanting to change lots before doing so I might have believed he was building this house for us but he did not discuss it with me. That proved to me that he was building this house strictly for money as an investment, not for us as a couple or a family. It also proved that he did not value my input or my feelings.

The controlling behaviour escalated as we had to make changes to the house plans to fit this new lot and he would get angry when our blueprint designer would agree with my ideas. I began wondering if changing my address was worth becoming a kept woman who should just sit there and look pretty. I was too worn out already to get entangled in more power struggles. I witnessed what his temper could really be when he slammed the table in a fit of rage in the middle of our final meeting with the blueprint designer. I walked away leaving him to build his house, his way, with *my* best friends. Ouch.

I was losing more and more reason every day to be proud of my life. How could I expect anyone else to be proud of me?

As I walked away I felt like I was jumping off the bridge but as desperate as I was to be saved, I was not desperate enough to be controlled. I would suffer continuing to pay the price of loneliness instead of paying the controlling price for luxury on the Boardwalk.

PART III

AGGRAVATING FACTOR
FIGHT #2

FILE #005566

*"Common sense is so rare these days it should
be classified as a super power."*
-Anonymous

CHAPTER 35
Take a Ride on the Crazy Train

It was the spring of 2015 and I had not heard anymore from RECA since April 2014. Even Carolyn Hackett from Libertas Property Management had backed off from negotiating the purchase of my portfolio. I had actually started to let my guard down thinking they had finally forgotten about me and it was the only silver lining for me to embrace while I suffered from a major heart break.

I had been getting some new clients referred to me for tenant placements that was supplementing the loss of residual monthly income I was experiencing due to more clients selling. It seemed like I might be able to overcome this online slandering by RECA just by continuing to provide excellent service to my clients and earning referrals from them.

I had a repeat client come to me who would always call on me for tenant placement services only. It was one of my favourite carriage condo properties for its tasteful and decorative renovation and floorplan and I had been lucky enough to always easily place good tenants, until this time around.

I had received an email response to one of my ads from a guy who responded with an overzealous description of himself and his business. He was a red flag to me right away but I was not getting much for responses and I wanted to do a test showing to see how this present tenant was maintaining the unit.

My spidey senses tingled again when I met him for a showing and my gut instincts warned me that this guy looked as desperate as his email inquiry reply sounded. He wanted to start negotiating new renovations in exchange for free rent and only wanted a six month lease now vs one year. He came across as very demanding. I let him know he should be looking for a place that would satisfy his needs better yet he demanded an application. I decided it was in my best interests not to deny him that so I handed him an application as we headed back to the parking lot and instructed him to email it to me. Well, then he claimed to not have a computer and wanted to complete it while sitting in my truck. As if! I'm sure he noticed the alarm in my face and my gut told me to tread carefully. I suggested he complete it in his own truck and scan it to me from his phone.

I expressed my need to get back to St. Albert in time for another appointment and the guy would not let me go without ensuring I had photo pictures of his new work contracts to prove the income he would be getting.

I was nervous but had to appear cool and collected and cooperative. I agreed to review his application with the owner and hightailed it out of that parking lot praying he would not follow me. I also prayed I would find a quality tenant before having to deal with this guy again.

This guy was relentless in hounding me with text messages and voicemails that indicated emotional instability. One message would show desperate interest in renting this unit and the next would be a complaint about the fact that I required cash for a security deposit and 1st month's rent. I had not even approved him so why was he even concerning himself with my processes?!

I advised him that I had found a more suitable tenant expecting he would disappear. NOT. I knew my world would come crashing down again when he texted me screen shots of the administrative penalty letter that he found on the RECA website. This letter showed my full business name, my personal name, and my complete home address.

This guy now knew where I lived because of RECA. I had every reason to believe that my family and I were going to be in danger. I was also on full guard and defense mode awaiting the harassment that would soon follow from RECA again.

St. Albert RCMP redirected me to Edmonton Police to file my harassment complaint because the business activities surrounding the harassing occurrences involved an Edmonton property address. Great. So I finally managed to file an Edmonton Police report file # 15227425 on June 6, 2015 and the constable I spoke with assisted me with a 'cease contact" notice to send to this psycho. **Interesting to note here how I am forced to file my complaint or claim in the appropriate jurisdiction but RECA is not.**

After advising him of the police report I filed and to back off, this guy starts leaving notes on the unit door for the present tenant to contact him with owner information so he could rent this unit without my involvement AND then, wait for it… The present tenant there called to notify me that he found her on Facebook trying again to get the owner's information to rent the place. He obviously went through her mail in her mailbox to get her name. Holy shit, what a psycho! Crazy people like this are just one more reason why there are always owners who are willing to pay someone like me.

Before I had the chance to notify the owner of what was going on, he called me regarding the call he received from the condo management company about the calls they received from this disgruntled renter. Tyson had complained about the "unlicensed property manager working for that unit". Unbelievable.

Of course, the owners always knew I was not a licensed property manager and supported me fully and, in turn, chose to call this guy and kindly ask him to back down. Well, that just led to six more harassing messages from him to the owner about me not being licensed. He made statements that I had agreed to rent to him and should allow him a move-in date of that Saturday. The present tenant was not even moving out for 2 more weeks! Who did this guy think he was fooling? As if the owner, or I, was going to budge.

I had to ask the constable who I filed my harassment complaint with to contact this lunatic himself and advise him to stay clear of anyone related to this property. Although that stopped further harassment from him, it did not erase the dark cloud of fear and anxiety that my daughter and I were still under knowing that our personal home address was splashed online for every other disgruntled tenant to find.

CHAPTER 36
Go Back 3 Spaces

The voicemails from Tricia Hickey at RECA started rolling in on June 12, 2015 asking if I "was still blatantly breaking the law…" as they had received another complaint.

I was going to be harassed again because of my exemplary service in protecting my client from the unsatisfactory renter. I was so insulted and at my wits end with this woman's condescending demeanor and lack of common sense. How could this organization, that regulates the real estate industry, give a rat's ass about a tenant who was not approved for rental accommodation?! Here I was again working in another cycle of emails defending myself when I, AGAIN, did nothing wrong. Karma was definitely confused.

From: Sly Solutions [mailto:sylvia@slysolutions.ca]
Sent: June-15-15 8:03 AM
To: Tricia Hickey
Subject: Tyson ▇▇▇▇▇▇

Tricia,

In response to your voice messages on June 12, 2015 please note that I am very aware of the complaint made by Tyson ▮▮▮▮▮ who can hardly be regarded as a reliable or valid complainant. He is a disgruntled guy obviously having a hard time being approved for rental accommodation and sticking it to me for not renting to him either. I had filed an Edmonton Police report (file # 15227425) on June 6, 2015 against Tyson due to his continued harassment of me, the owners, and the present tenant. The owners of the unit are acquaintances of mine from Vermillion and asked me to help them. The tenant chosen for their unit is also a long term family friend of mine (my Step Father's first wife!) and can easily be proven.

There are plenty of rentals in the Edmonton area for Tyson to choose from yet he ignored my suggestion, and the owners, to back off and search for accommodation elsewhere even though I notified him of the police report and that he could be charged with a criminal offense for continuing to contact me or the owners, directly, or indirectly. I have documented proof of all communications between Tyson and the owners and between Tyson and myself, with proof of deceit from Tyson, for my police report.

I have not been advertising my services anywhere since 2013 and have rapidly lost my portfolio due to RECA being successful in defacing the good reputation I had earned and held for 11 years for simply helping them find quality tenants. I'm not swindling anybody. I simply protected these owners from a poor tenant choice and it seems I now have grounds and fair reason for following through with filing criminal charges against Tyson ▮▮▮▮▮.

Sylvia Germain

From: Tricia Hickey
Sent: Monday, June 15, 2015 9:26 AM
To: Sly Solutions
Subject: RE:

Hi Sylvia,

I'm sorry to hear you had a disgruntled applicant. I think it is very clear that you are not swindling anyone and that you are running an effective business. Unfortunately, at the time you started the business you may, or may not have been aware, that the business structure you offered clients required a license. And I understand, after years of running a business, how do you suddenly stop that business to try and get licensed, which takes time and money. How are you supposed to maintain your business while getting into compliance, without losing all your clients? I understand that. I understand the feat seems impossible. However there are ways for you to do it but you need to work with us to get in you into compliance.

Unfortunately, even though the advertisement has now been removed, the advertisement was still up and it advertised a property for rent that you were not the owner of. This, as you are aware, constitutes a trade in real estate and requires a license.

If you have changed your business model to get into compliance then I have the following questions:

1. Why was this property advertised this way?

2. How zdo you now find tenants for your clients?

3. What did you change in your business to get into compliance with the *Real Estate Act*?

Thank you

Tricia Hickey
Senior Professional Conduct Review Officer
Professional Standards Unit
thickey@reca.ca

From: Sly Solutions [mailto:sylvia@slysolutions.ca]
Sent: June-17-15 11:21 AM
To: Tricia Hickey
Subject: Re:

I do appreciate your demonstration of understanding my position however I question...

1. Why would I pay fees to start licensing with an industry/organization that has already assassinated both my business name and personal name to the point of no return? Seriously Tricia, would you?? Maybe I would be willing to commence licensing this week if RECA could assure me that they would "work with me" by reversing the "REVOKED" status of the A+ rating with the BBB for Sly Solutions Ltd and to wave the administrative penalty splashed all over the internet. I don't trust that the education department will even cooperate in qualifying me to even commence licensing given our tangled history.

2. Why is RECA arguing the point that I am directly employed as an agent by these owners?

3. Why has it been written in the Exemption Regulation of your Real Estate Act that an employee of a non-profit organization is granted the exemption to do what I do without licensing? What makes those employees more qualified to advertise a unit for rent and less of a risk to the public? It just so happens that I do have clients who operate non-profit organizations (including a pastor). Based on this non-profit clause it appears as though I should be able to start a non-profit organization with a partner to help the homeless and hire Sly Solutions Ltd as an employee to find them rental accommodation while also helping investors find renters so I will look into that further with my lawyer.

You do not govern me and I have never posed as a licensed anything and you have never had a valid complaint against my tenant placement services. Your interrogations and assassination of me are not justified. You have splashed my personal name and business name with my home address all over the internet which has not only infringed on privacy acts but exposing my home address has caused a great concern for my safety with the proven disgruntled Tyson ██████████ that RECA seems to have empowered. This psycho has texted me proof that he has my address from your website and has gone to the extent of illegally going through the mail of the current tenant at address ██████████ ██ and found her on Facebook yesterday and is now harassing her. I have never provided my home address on a business card or on my website now **please remove my personal information from your sites.**

From: Tricia Hickey
Sent: Wednesday, June 17, 2015 1:43 PM
To: Sly Solutions
Subject: RE:

Hi Sylvia,

In order for me to answer your questions I need to address some things in the beginning. We are a regulatory body that governs the *Real Estate Act*. The *Real Estate Act* is an Act passed by the Government of Alberta. In the Act it defines what a trade in real estate is, and if someone is trading in real estate in Alberta, they require a license.

The Real Estate Council of Alberta enforces the Real Estate Act. If someone is trading in real estate while unauthorized we attempt to work with that person to get them into compliance. If an individual chooses not to work with us then an Administration Penalty is issued. The Administration Penalty is a form of discipline used to deter someone from continuing their actions, that are in breach of the law. Our mandate is to protect consumers and to provide services that enhance and improve the industry and the business of industry members. *(I AM providing an enhanced service to the public that poses no risk to them!)* In order to protect consumers we post Administration Penalties on the internet for the public to view. The government has determined it is in the public's best interest to have individuals who trade in real estate be licensed. Unfortunately, you are trading in real estate and are not licensed.

In our last file, you were very defensive and eventually chose not to cooperate with us. Since you chose to not cooperate with us we were left with no choice but to issue you an Administrative Penalty. *How did I not cooperate?*

To answer your questions:

1. "Why would I pay fees to start licensing with an industry/organization..." Because you are currently trading in real estate without a license, which is what you were fined for in the past. You obviously love what you do. If you get into compliance then you can advertise your business and gain more customers, and we will not contact you for trading while unauthorized. ... that has already assassinated both my business name and personal name to the point of no return? You refused to cooperate with an investigation and the consequences were an Administrative Penalty and the public being aware of the penalty. By the way, the Administration Penalty gets removed from the internet after 2 years. **I never refused to cooperate with their investigation. I answered all their questions in great detail in my first response letter in February 2013**.

2. "Why is RECA arguing the point that I am directly employed as an agent by these owners?" In order to be an employee of the owners, the owners would need to be filing with CRA that you are their employee. **Who exactly defines this? My clients come to me and enter a fair business contract with me to hire my agent services for a monthly fee. CRA filing is redundant here. Are they doing that? If yes, provide evidence of this as you may be exempt from the Act if you are an employee.**

3. "Why has it been written in the Exemption Regulation of your Real Estate Act that an employee of a non-profit organization is granted the exemption to do what I do without licensing? What makes those employees more qualified to advertise a unit for rent and less of a risk to the public?" If you are an employee of the owner of the business, then you are working on behalf of the owner. The owner has the right to buy and sell real estate without a license. In your case, the owners are trusting you and hiring you as a third party to do a job. This is what moves you into our jurisdiction. **Huh? This does not even answer my question nor does it make sense. Again, what does buying and selling real estate by the owner have to do with me handling residential renters?**

4. "You do not govern me and I have never posed as a licensed anything and you have never had a valid complaint against my tenant placement services." We do govern your actions when you are trading in real estate without a license. It doesn't matter if you feel a complaint is valid or not. The simple fact is you are trading in real estate, which requires a license. Laws are in place to prevent harm from occurring to the public. **I trade in residential tenancies NOT real estate. The nature of the complaint DOES have to be divulged according to the natural laws of justice.**

It is much easier to work with us than against us. Because as long as you continue to trade in real estate without a license, we will have no choice but continue our investigations. In extreme cases, where someone is unauthorized and continues to trade in real estate while unauthorized, and has been warned by us that they require a license, we will take the case to the courts and get a Court Ordered Injunction.

Here's the bottom line. You honestly seem like you run a really good, effective business. You were naturally very defensive when we last spoke and you let your defences get the best of the situation. Unfortunately those defences had consequences. If you work with us we will work with you. You are obviously continuing to run your business so let's find a way to get you into compliance. Then you can advertise your business and gain more customers.

Sincerely,
Tricia Hickey
Senior Professional Conduct Review Officer
Professional Standards Unit
thickey@reca.ca

Geeze, I did not realize that "laws were in place to prevent harm to the public..." Where was the law to protect me from the harm that this organization was inflicting on me?! This girl was talking to me like I was 10 years old and I was probably 20 years older than her. I was not even going to waste my words re-examining her on her answers with the notes I made here in bold. I needed to change the direction of this game...

CHAPTER 37
Ring A-Round the Rosie
Education Dance

I had absolutely no intention of being governed by this ring of bullies by handing money to them for fees on courses that did not pertain to my business activities. I was, however, going to test this gal to see how much they were really willing to work with me. You will notice that I do not receive any simple "yes or no" answers…there is almost 50 shades of grey here in Tricia's responses that she explains as "difficult…because I am overlapping in numerous departments" and there are "tricky parts"…Of course there are.

Why is RECA so worthy of grey areas and "tricky parts" yet I am only allowed black and white "yes or no" explanations? Through all of these long winded responses **I still did not get clear answers as to what exactly was expected of me to be "in compliance".** Will you see a clear answer…?

From: Sly Solutions [mailto:sylvia@slysolutions.ca]
Sent: June-19-15 10:05 AM
To: Tricia Hickey
Subject: Re:

Tricia,

Can you please clarify what "get into compliance" really means? Does this mean that I can appease this situation by registering and commencing the on line course or does this mean that I will continue to be harassed and/or penalized until I have the chance to complete ALL the courses (which could take 2-3 years)?

Can you also confirm that I would not be further harassed or charged with "unauthorized trading as a real estate broker" if I actually satisfied the $5000 administrative penalty?

Thank-you,
Sylvia Germain

From: Tricia Hickey
Sent: Friday, June 19, 2015 11:00 AM
To: Sly Solutions
Subject: RE:

Well...these are difficult for me to answer because you are overlapping into numerous departments. I am in the compliance department. You have a collections department issue and you would need to speak with licensing and education. So this is what I have done so far...

I just went and spoke with the collections department and explained that you are the lady, who is running a good business, freaked out when we called and unfortunately you ended up with a $5,000 penalty, however I explained our ultimate goal is to get you into compliance, and you appear to be interested in cooperating with us. They agreed and agreed to halt collections on you at this time, IF you start getting yourself into compliance and you continue working with us. (I say continue because I feel like your email below is big progress).

To get into compliance. This is difficult to answer. However a first step is to register for the education courses that you will need. We know that the course takes a minimum of 8 months to complete and we know that you cannot complete the course overnight. Technically we cannot say, just complete the course, and we will turn a blind eye in the meantime. Technically we cannot say that because you are currently trading in real estate which breaks the law. However showing us that you are trying to get into compliance shows us you take it seriously and you want to continue in your line of work, this can result in a mitigating factor being applied to your file.

Here is the tricky part. In order to become a broker, you have to be a licensed real estate associate for 2 years. In order to run the brokerage you need to be a broker. You can be the owner of a brokerage, and hire a licensed broker to oversee the licensed portion of your job for those 2 years, until you can qualify to become a broker. If you want to try and make an exception on this...you would need to speak with the Registrar, who is Joseph Fernandez. I do not know if an exception can be made on this.

From a compliance side. If you proceed to try and get into compliance then yes that will appease this situation. But I want to be straight up on this. If you do start to get into compliance and start your education requirements and we close this file, but then I receive a new complaint. According to the Act, I must look into the file. But we will not be searching you out to see if you are in compliance or not. We move on complaint submissions or information received.

I hope this helps.

Tricia Hickey
Senior Professional Conduct Review Officer
Professional Standards Unit

From: Sly Solutions [mailto:sylvia@slysolutions.ca]
Sent: July-09-15 2:17 PM
To: Tricia Hickey
Subject: Education question

Tricia, I did receive information from education services regarding the Property Management course. However, you are asking me to "comply" by investing my time and money in a full-fledged realtor and broker education. I'm still not clear as to why the expectation for education is this high in my situation. It really is equivalent to penalizing a legal secretary for not spending years completing the entire gamut of law courses and acting as a lawyer and Supreme Court judge before acting as a legal secretary. It seems completely unreasonable.

Will RECA be satisfied if I complete just the Property Management portion?

Sylvia Germain

Can you send me what they sent you? Have you asked them questions about what it would take to get you into compliance as a property manager only?

Tricia Hickey
Senior Professional Conduct Review Officer
Professional Standards Unit
thickey@reca.ca

Wow. I was seriously pulling my hair out by this time. Did this girl have cauliflower between her ears? RECA had for 2 years branded me as guilty of acting as a real estate broker and Tricia Hickey had been demanding I refrain from broker activities. Now, she is acting as though a property management course might be all I require. Who the hell was calling all these shots on me? Tricia Hickey? Education department? Bob Myroniuk? Collections? This was the most disorganized organization, ever.

July 13, 2015

Hi Sylvia,

I requested the email communication with you from education and see that back in 2013 you tried to qualify for the exemption, however you did not meet the requirements.

Can you please advise what your plans are? Are you planning on enrolling in the course? Are you looking for a licensed real estate broker? Etc.

Thank you

Tricia Hickey
Senior Professional Conduct Review Officer
Audits & Investigations
Real Estate Council of Alberta (RECA)

From: Tricia Hickey
Sent: July-15-15 10:37 AM
To: Shelly Sherstobitoff
Subject: RE: Sylvia Germain

What courses does Sylvia Germain need to take to become a licensed property manager? And what is the cost of each of those courses? And approximate time length?

Thanks,
Tricia

From: education inbox
Sent: July-15-15 11:37 AM
To: Tricia Hickey
Subject: RE: Sylvia Germain

Hi,

She needs to take the following courses:

- **Fundamentals of Real Estate (approximately 200 hours of online content)**

This RECA course provides you with a wide range of foundational information related to the real estate profession. As the pre-requisite course, the *Fundamentals of Real Estate* provides you with the knowledge and skills needed for the Practice courses and ultimately for your real estate or property management practice. The course is online which offers you easy and convenient access regardless of your location or time availability. The course fee is **$1500**, which includes access to the online course, support from the Education Helpdesk, 2 course manuals, 2 practice exams, 1 mid-term exam fee, and 1 final exam fee. The course fee must be paid when you enroll. The exams are delivered at authorized exam centres and you are responsible for the exam proctoring fees.

- **Practice of Property Management (approximately 70hours of online content)**

This RECA course provides the basic knowledge and skills needed for a career in property management. It covers such topics as leasing, tenant selection, relevant legislation, property operations, residential tenancies and trust accounting. The course is online which offers you easy and convenient access regardless of your location or time availability. The course fee is **$1500**, which includes access to the online course, support from the Education Helpdesk, the course manual, and 1 final exam fee. The course fee must be paid when you enroll. The exam is delivered at authorized exam centres and you are responsible for the exam proctoring fees.

Ok, so back in October 2013 the education department emailed me a very lengthy denial to my education exemption request that advised I was required to complete these 2 courses PLUS work under another brokerage firm for 2 years before enrolling in brokerage licensing courses. Now, this gal from the education department claims these 2 courses might suffice. **I kept getting conflicting information.**

There was no clarity here as to what was expected for me to "comply" so what was I supposed to do? I still didn't want to work within their business model. My clients wanted my landlord agent business model, not theirs.

*"No, I really am not a smart ass. I am a skilled
professional in pointing out the obvious."*
-Anonymous

CHAPTER 38
A Knock-Out!

I had to get a strong legal defense to support me in a courtroom where I could end this game once and for all. The lawyer I had been dealing with had recently been on a radio segment discussing regulatory law. It was evident that he supported that corporate side of regulatory law very strongly. I knew that he believed I was being bullied yet I became concerned that he would be subconsciously biased in having my back. I did not want to be invoiced for another call to him and I began pounding the internet for other lawyers who could give me a fresh opinion.

I came across Darin ████████ who specialized in quasi criminal regulatory and administrative cases. He agreed that I had an obvious harassment case but suggested it would be in my best interest, financially, to wait to use my defense in the event that RECA actually tried to prosecute me. It could easily cost me $25,000 to initiate against RECA and they might not get more than a slap on the wrist. Although I did not want to wait for them to try and prosecute me, it did make more sense to me.

I also sought legal counsel with Ronald ████████ at the office of McLennan Ross. I provided him with a reference copy of my five pages of chronological order of events. Before even finishing the first page he looked up at me over his glasses and concluded with the word "Extortion".

Finally! A lawyer who was not afraid to call it what it was. He threw out approximate costs of closer to $10,000 and $15,000 versus $25,000. Well, that was just only slightly more comforting. I was really impressed though when I saw that he had already done some homework before I got there. He pointed out that section 17, Regulation of Business of an Industry Member, of the Real Estate Act refers to authorization required for "real estate brokers, mortgage brokers and real estate appraisers" and does not include the statement that they have authorization to regulate landlord agents OR property managers. There you have it. That seemed pretty clear.

I was sure I had discussed that defense with one of the 'mean girls' at some point and I guess I would have to mention that in writing, again. I would still wait for RECA to make the legal move for me to defend versus me initiating legal action and I would continue having my own back.

My google search for cases against RECA brought up interesting information on www.PrivateSectorAct.com showing that there had been a history of others with complaints against RECA who were looking for justice. It did not look very legit, however, and my email inquiry for a contact name and number led me nowhere.

All I could do for now, again, was politely tell Tricia Hickey and RECA to fuck off.

July 14, 2015 11:50 AM

Tricia,

I do not love what I do. I hate what I do (which is why I considered selling out to Libertas in the first place) so why would I invest all this time and money to continue it on a bigger scale when I still won't get any reprieve from you or hope of clearing my business name? After all my attempts to qualify for exemptions I don't trust Joseph Fernandez will offer any exemption hope either.

You've already told me that you will never be willing to consider my "effective" and sought after landlord agent business model as exempt based on my numerous and reasonable pleas of:

> 1) The on-site manager exemption even though these are the same responsibilities and that I've dealt with many "on-site managers" who do not live on-site and that your interpretation is not binding by law

OR

2) The "direct employee of an owner" clause even though I file both personal and corporate taxes with the CRA and that the meaning of "direct employee" is blurred and, again, only interpreted by you

OR

3) The government AND other reputable education that I have to independently operate a business

AND/OR

4) The 12 satisfactory years under my belt (that would typically be considered Grandfathered) without one valid service complaint or need to ever refer to The Real Estate Act or use your resources

Along with the fact that **I DO NOT hold or control owner rent income and expenses, or owner budgets or do property value analysis.** What risk am I even posing to my clients if I do not manage their rent and operating expenses and do not make decisions without owner direction and have the owner billed directly by service providers for any repairs done hum?

And...that I will continue to be harassed for at least the 3 or 4 years it takes to get some broker title even though I have never ever posed as a realtor or broker or want to be one. That's equivalent to penalizing a legal secretary for not spending years completing the entire gamut of law courses and acting as a lawyer and Supreme Court judge before acting as a legal secretary. It is completely unreasonable.

I **DID** cooperate fully in disclosing my unique business model and practices. And, like I said before, I cooperated in not advertising for 2 years and allowed my portfolio to dwindle to nothing.

Your section 17 of the Act that you regulate and requires authorization does not refer to trading in real estate as a Property Manager or Landlord Agent. It refers to acting as a real estate broker, a mortgage broker or a real estate appraiser which I have not done. I have been unreasonably interrogated and penalized based on "vexatious" complaints.

I have been seeking other reputable employment and I have also found new reputable legal counsel. If I'm not successful in securing new employment because of my slandered name on the internet I will be inclined to come after you and Libertas Property Management for extortion, unreasonable defamation of character, undue harassment, disrespecting my privacy by inappropriately splashing my personal home address on your site, and court costs. Now, unless you have a reasonable reason to investigate me further please do not contact me again in any form, directly or indirectly.

Sylvia Germain

From: Tricia Hickey
Sent: July-22-15 3:55 PM
To: 'sylvia@slysolutions.ca'
Subject: Sylvia Germain

Hi Sylvia,

Though I do have sympathy for your situation, the fact is you have already been fined for breaching the Real Estate Act. Instead of taking the necessary education requirements to become licensed, you reduced your advertising, yet you continued to do activities that required a license. I messaged our education department to inquire what you would need to become licensed and the cost. It appears the approximate cost is $3,000. Your Administration Penalty is $5,000.

I am going to close this investigation with a Warning Letter. The Warning Letter outlines that if you trade in real estate again, while unauthorized, we will issue you a much steeper fine than the $5,000 that you were issued before. You are trading in real estate without a license and you are required to have a license.

My suggestion during this time is to speak with the person handling collections, Andrew Bone, and see if you can work out some sort of compromise to start you on the path of getting licensed.

Sincerely,

Tricia Hickey
Senior Professional Conduct Review Officer
Professional Standards Unit
thickey@reca.ca

17 July 2015

Private and Confidential

Case: 005225

Sylvia Germain
Sly Solutions Ltd.

Dear Ms. Germain:

Warning Letter: Activities Require Authorization

The Real Estate Council of Alberta (RECA) administers the *Real Estate Act* (Act). The Act requires individuals conducting certain activities to hold a licence.

Based on information received, RECA has determined your activities required a licence. You advertised a property you did not own, on behalf of owners, to find a tenant. This requires a license.

You have previously been fined by RECA for trading while unauthorized. You appear to have adjusted your business by minimizing your business advertising. The business advertising no longer advertises services that require a license. While you do not advertise services that require a license, you did advertise a property that you did not own. This was clearly outlined to you in our last investigation such activity is considered trading in real estate and requires a license.

You were warned and fined by RECA previously. In this case, we are only issuing you a Warning Letter because of your cooperation. Furthermore, you have demonstrated willingness to adjust your business model to get into compliance.

Ultimately, you have two options. Either you cease all trading in real estate, or get licensed to trade in real estate.

This is a formal warning that you are not authorized to trade in real estate as a real estate broker in Alberta. You are expected to refrain from these activities until you become authorized by RECA.

Should RECA receive evidence of future unauthorized activity, the matter will not be treated leniently. The Act provides for fines up to $25,000.00 for unauthorized activity.

If you require the legislation supporting this decision or have any other questions, please contact Tricia Hickey, Senior Professional Conduct Review Officer, at 403-685-7942 or thickey@reca.ca.

Yours truly,

Bob Myroniuk,
Executive Director

*"I have decided I no longer want to be an adult so, if anyone
needs me I'll be in my blanket fort colouring."*
-Anonymous

CHAPTER 39
Defamed & Unemployable

Every time I considered selling my portfolio to someone else I was still left with unanswered questions as to what I would do to replace the residual income I was accustomed to having. There was no job out there that would come close to paying me the amount of monthly income I had built up, with or without a university degree.

I no longer had the mental capacity or energy to exercise my creative skills in creating a new business idea for myself. I tried to convince myself I would have to be happy with a 9-5 moo cow job that would give me minimal 2 weeks annual vacation time, health insurance benefits, and just enough salary to pay the bills, along with higher levels of rush hour driving stress, and office politics. I was really just trying to leave one rat race for another rat race. I had to do something. I had to let the universe know I was open to new options.

Over the summer of 2015 I spent as much time as I could looking for new job opportunities, submitting resumes and cover letters. I had assistance from my neighbour who was a head hunter but there just was not a match for me. After at least 30 dead end job applications that I was well qualified for I knew I was wasting my time. I didn't get a single interview.

I was middle aged and had been self-employed for too long to have any employer look at me seriously. I was not trainable or an ideal team player in the eyes of anyone hiring because I had been working for myself more than 10 years. I was also under educated for everything I was experienced enough to do. On-line job application formats did not care about evening courses at NAIT or my Credit Union accreditations. I had to tick off University degree or simple High School. I did not have a University degree so these systems already had me set up to fail for any position above entry level.

Job connections through my clients were not feasible either as the majority of my clients were out of town, out of province, or out of country.

I did come across an investor through a friend who was extremely interested in my portfolio as well as my business model. I was ready to sell it off but when he heard that my client list had shrunk from a $100,000/year revenue to $60,000/year he decided not to go forward with it. He was looking for at least a $100,000 in revenue to start with to give him wiggle room for client drop offs. That made sense.

Just as I had given up all hope, my ex-husband called me with an offer. Bless his soul. He empathized with my situation and had talked to the bank manager he knew quite well at his Scotiabank branch about my situation and my financial industry back ground plus my willingness to get back into the banking industry. She welcomed my resume and set me up with an interview at a different branch, 45 minutes away, for a Small Business Advisor.

I could not imagine myself driving that every day both ways in rush hour traffic as that 45 minutes would be one hour minimum each way but I also could not imagine living in the vice grip of RECA for another year.

I was pretty sure I had nailed all the hard questions in the job interview. Until one of the interviewers mentioned the government sanction against my business showing online. There was a concern about how their business customers would take my advice seriously if they became aware of that black mark against me. What could I say? There was just no climbing out of this rabbit hole.

I might not hire someone with that black mark for a position like that either.

CHAPTER 40
Health Benefits Challenge

In November 2015 I received a letter from Sun Life Insurance threatening to exclude me from a long list of medications. The medications I had claimed in the past 2 years for shingles, chest infections, ear infection, eye infection, sinus infection, boils, and sleeping pills was a red flag to them. I was accused of not disclosing pre-existing conditions and allergies on my insurance application in 2013. Lovely.

As I mentioned earlier in Chapter 35, I had been a pro-active healthy person. Previous to 2013 I had one antibiotic prescription in February 2010 and one in May 2009. Between 2013 and 2015 I had claimed over 10 different prescriptions. In fact a tally of my health store receipts proves I spent $1123.82 in 2013 in homeopathic remedies aside from those prescriptions. These prescriptions and purchases were not related to pre-existing conditions or allergies. They were not basic vitamin supplements either. They were all related to a weakened immune system, digestive disturbances and hormonal disturbances caused by chronic stress.

This slap in the face from Sun Life was only increasing that chronic stress and I was not going to be bullied by this corporate monster either. I went straight to the top this time and filed an initial complaint with OLHI, Ombud Service for Life Health Insurance in Ontario. The representative I shared my verbal complaint with over the phone said that this was a rare occurrence and definitely did not sound fair. He was more than willing to direct me in exactly what to write and who to write it to. I'm grateful for his genuine concern and help. I wished there could be an Ombud Service for RECA. Service Alberta certainly wasn't effective.

It took me 6 months of letter writing and retrieving medical history letters from my doctor before Sun Life finally backed down and realized they had accused me in error. I was so grateful for my doctor and all her assistance and compassion with the strains I was under.

I did not want to continue a relationship with Sun Life but I really did not have a better option. I now had a long list of pre-existing conditions that made it too costly, and almost impossible, to get approved by any other health insurance provider. By the time I finally won the battle against Sun Life I was ready to cave into anti-depressants.

RECA had effectively branded a white collar criminal. I could not get anyone to hire me for a job. I rarely left my house to be able to meet any man at all, and my monthly revenue was now less than half of what it was in 2012. PLUS, I was getting screwed out of health benefits.

Based on what I believe about Karma I will never understand why the world seemed to be conspiring against me. I was a good person, always doing onto others as I would have them do unto me. What had I done so wrong? It had to be because I was under so much pressure of negativity that I could not believe that there really is always a sun behind the clouds. The more I dwelled in my self-pity the more shit came my way. The law of attraction; it's so real.

PART IV

AGGRAVATING FACTOR
FIGHT #3

FILE #005566

CHAPTER 41
Paranoia Will Destroy Ya

On November 19, 2015, a few days after receiving the Sun Life exclusion threats, I received another wonderful gift from another new gal at RECA, Nancy Iwasiw, with the subject "Notice of New Investigation…"

2015-11-19 4:31 PM

Good Afternoon Ms. Germain,

I have attached a PDF copy (138898.pdf) of the letter sent today to your last confirmed address (20 Oakridge Dr. N, St. Albert, AB, T8N 6H8). This letter has been sent by registered mail.

Please confirm receipt of this email.

Regards,

Nancy Iwasiw
Professional Conduct Review Officer

I ignored the email. I ignored everything. In fact, I stopped getting out of bed in the mornings now and ignored most of my emails. I ignored the registered mail notice. I did not go anywhere anymore. I did not get dressed. I did not even shower most days. I ignored my telephone and, of course, my doorbell. I did not see my daughter off to school. I did manage to put clothes on when I absolutely had to for groceries or property showings but that was rare. I never did my hair or make-up anymore.

I was a hopeless disgrace living only to be a punching bag for others. I prayed so hard for understanding. Why was I being battered by life? How strong was one little single mom supposed to be? I had been tested all my life to build strength and I just did not have it anymore. I did not feel like I was ever going to contribute to a worthy purpose again. This black hole was like quick sand pulling me deeper down every day. Every time I believed my luck would turn around someone else was tugging at me. Clients, tenants, RECA, Sun Life, etc. Even Passport Canada gave me a hard time when renewing my daughter's passport. I had to resend supporting divorce documents that I had already provided the officer in person. That person did not provide them to the ivory tower. My patience could not be tested anymore. It just couldn't.

Every morning I awoke, I wished I was dead. Every night I went to bed, tossing and turning, even with sleeping pills. I wished I would die in the night. I thought about writing up a will and getting ducks in a row and considering that the sleeping pills would be the best way. I was believing my daughter would be better off without me and that I wouldn't be missed much anyway because I was so miserable being alive. I had no purpose to contribute to anymore.

I had to remind myself that it was my daughter that gave me reason to stay alive. I could not leave her in life with the burden of a mother who committed suicide. I remembered the pain my high school boyfriend endured when his father committed suicide after losing his business and wife. I felt so guilty knowing I was providing such a poor example for my girl yet I could not pull myself out.

Even though I knew pills could not change my circumstances, my doctor believed they would help me cope better to live more normally again. I tried the pills but didn't receive the magic.

January 7, 2016 Nancy Iwasiw emails me again about registered mail being returned and this time she notes a property address as a reference to the new complaint...

It was the first time any of those Professional Conduct Review Officers had actually complied with their own regulations. She divulged at least some information regarding who the complainant was, but there still was not any information as to what the actual complaint was. I knew what it was though.

This property address had been sold by the owner in August 2015 and the tenants were ruffled about having to move. I remember them giving the owners realtor a hard time about showings and the realtor needing my assistance with them.

I had done everything by the book, (the Residential Tenancies Act book) in providing proper 90 day notice to these tenants, providing a thorough cleaning list, 24 hr notice for realtor showings, a thorough sign out inspection, and provided a detailed deposit refund for the owner to return their full deposit. I wrote kind wishes to them in their new home and even cut them some slack on their refusal to have the carpets "professionally steam cleaned" as per the cleaning list. They self-cleaned the carpets and if I had new tenants coming in I would have charged them for a "professional steam cleaning" but seeing as the unit was being sold I let it go.

The tenants had been renting that unit for 3 years and after the 1st year always had excuses for not being able to lock in and had to go month to month. Upon having to collect a batch of new post-dated cheques for the owner I had advised the tenant that the owner would likely consider selling if they did not wish to sign a lease term. They would not see the fairness in that.

During their tenancy I had coordinated new carpet, new toilets, new faucets, new lino, and replaced dryer knobs for free. I never left an issue unsettled. They had no reason to file a complaint against me whatsoever and were just wanting to stick it to someone for making them move.

A simple google of my business name gave them the ammunition to stick it to me. For nothing. I had gone above and beyond for these tenants with notes of praise from both the owner and their realtor for my service and my efforts yet this is what I got from the tenants.

My back was up higher than it could get but I refused to get tangled in this bullshit again. This was not an investigation about me keeping anybody's money or trying to sell a property or calling myself a broker. This was just more vexatious BULLSHIT!!!

RECA's black marks against me were being compounded by their online defamation of me, not by my service or my actions. They could waste all the time they had chasing me and writing letters but I was not wasting my time on them. I was too busy frying other fish trying to save my health benefits. RECA would have to wait. I headed to Mexico for stress leave.

CHAPTER 42
COURT ORDER – Go To Jail, Do Not Pass Go, Do Not Collect $200

I had a fabulous time in Mexico and as my usual luck would have it, came home just in time to receive a Civil Claim Court Order for the $5000 administrative penalty. It was stamped with a file date of February 24, 2015 and I received it on February 23, 2016. They were hanging onto this order for a whole year, minus 1 day, choosing to harass me for that year instead of just serving me and getting it over with. Nice. What kind of strategy was that? I later learned that the statute of limitations allows only two years to claim penalties. This original administrative penalty was dated July 9, 2013. We were already beyond this two year limitation.

It was time to call my familiar lawyer, Brian ████████, again. He remembered my case and was surprised that this was still going on. I had not talked with him since the Fall of 2013 so, of course he thought it was done. I can't imagine what I would have paid in legal fees if I had approached him every time RECA barked. I really did need his help this time and by the grace of God, he assisted me, free of charge, with the dispute notes I needed to show these bullies just how far I would push back. I'm grateful for this Brian.

DISPUTE
SCHEDULE "A"

1. This Dispute Note is filed on behalf of Sylvia Germain, referred to hereinafter as the "Defendant."

2. Except as and where hereinafter expressly admitted, the Defendant denies each and every allegation in the civil claim.

3. At no time was the Defendant trading in real estate.

4. At no time did the Defendant act or portray herself as a real estate broker.

5. The company the Defendant works for, Sly Solutions Ltd. ("SSL"), acts as an agent for certain landlords. SSL is the party that holds all the contracts with landlords and which acts as a landlord's agent. Section 17 of The *Real Estate Act* authorizes the Plaintiff to regulate real estate brokers, mortgage brokers and real estate appraisers, but not independent agents of landlords.

6. The Plaintiff imposed an administrative penalty against Sylvia Germain when they were concerned about the independent business activities of SSL and accordingly, have named the wrong party in this action.

7. The administrative penalty was imposed and made public on-line without any valid hearing being held, nor were the rules of natural justice adhered to by the Plaintiff in imposing this administrative penalty against the wrong party.

8. Sylvia Germain was, at all relevant times, an employee of Sly Solutions Ltd., providing work and services to SSL. **The civil Claim discloses no cause of action** against Sylvia Germain whatsoever and insofar as it names her as a Defendant, the civil claim is frivolous, vexatious, and an abuse of the court's process. In this regard, Sylvia Germain seeks full indemnity, solicitor-and-own client cost against the Plaintiff.

9. Further, or in the alternative, if the Defendant is liable to the Plaintiff to any extent, which is not admitted but rather is expressly denied, then Sylvia Germain claims set-off from the Plaintiff, as more fully particularized in the Counterclaim appended hereto and marked as "Schedule B" and may rightfully appeal to Court of Queen's Bench to claim for further punitive damages in excess of the financial jurisdiction of the Provincial Court Civil.

10. The Defendant disputes and disagrees with the Plaintiff's choice of venue. The Defendant was employed by SSL for services in the Edmonton, Alberta and St. Albert, AB area, where SSL carries on business. The registered office of SSL is located in St. Albert, Alberta. The Defendant, Sylvia Germain, at all times relevant and material resides in St. Albert, Alberta.

The appropriate venue for the conduct of this Action is St. Albert, Alberta, and in this regard the Defendant expressly pleads and relies upon the provisions of the *Provincial Court Act*, R.S.A 2000, c. P-31, particularly Sections 27 and 28, and the *Provincial Court Civil Division Regulation*, Alta. Reg. 329/89, particularly Section 2.

WHEREFORE THE DEFENDANT, SYLVIA GERMAIN, REQUESTS THAT THE PLAINTIFF'S ACTION BE DISMISSED WITH COSTS ON A FULL INDEMNITY SOLICITOR-AND-OWN-CLIENT BASIS.

I should have laid money on the table to continue getting his assistance for the schedule B but with help from Google, I wrote up the schedule "B" myself. That mistake rears itself in the next book.

SCHEDULE "B"

1. Pecuniary damages for on-line public defamation of business character resulting in loss of revenue for Sly Solutions Ltd of $12,859 evident between 2013 year end income tax return and 2014 year end income tax return and a $24,523 loss of revenue between 2014 year end and 2015 year end income tax returns.

2. Punitive damages for loss of other employability due to on-line defamation of business and personal character by the Real Estate Council of Alberta.

3. Pecuniary damages for legal costs incurred in 2013 for mediation attempts made by Sylvia Germain and any further legal costs associated with the legal defense and counterclaim of this action.

4. Punitive damages for continuous unreasonable harassment since January 2013 by Real Estate Council of Alberta causing mental and physical distress to Sylvia Germain and family leading to RCMP intervention as well as unexpected medically recorded stress and heart related illnesses in 2013, 2014 and 2015 and therefore also resulting in medical coverage challenges with Sunlife.

5. Punitive damages for ongoing harassment by Real Estate Council of Alberta resulting from vexatious complaints to them from disgruntled tenants who become aware of this on-line defamation of personal and business character that continue to negatively affect Sylvia Germain and her family's quality of life.

March 23, 2016 I received notice that a pre-trial conference is scheduled for RECA vs. Sylvia Germain on November 24, 2016 at the Calgary Courts Centre and I am invited to participate by telephone. Calgary Court? What kind of bullshit is this now?!

Obviously dispute note #8 and #10 have been completely ignored. When I was filing a complaint against the psycho renter I had to go into Edmonton because "that's where the business took place", even though I lived in St. Albert and was concerned about my safety in my home. I am the defendant here so why does RECA get to conveniently file through the Calgary courts? That just wreaks double standards to me, and more money from me.

The silver lining I did find here was that my dispute notes were obviously considered "legitimate" or a pre-trial conference would not have been set at all. That was enough to give me hope.

"You never know how strong you are until being strong is the only choice you have."
-Bob Marley

CHAPTER 43
P...P...P...Put 'Em Up!

Nancy Iwasiw was continuing to send emails threatening more administrative penalties and now that I knew I was going to have the ability to tell my story in the courts, I was able to muster the energy to reply...

From: Nancy Iwasiw
Sent: Tuesday, April 5, 2016 11:23 AM
To: sylvia@slysolutions.ca
Subject: RECA will issue a penalty to you if you do not respond...

Good Morning Sylvia,

We have now made several attempts to contact you with respect to a complaint we received surrounding your unauthorized property management activities (RECA file 005566).

You have not responded to our Notice of an Investigation, which was sent by registered mail as well as by email on November 19, 2015. You refused to accept registered mail and have not responded to subsequent phone messages and email messages, the latest of which were sent and left by me on March 29, 2016.

This email is to advise that if you do not contact me by **April 15, 2016**, RECA will have no alternative but to issue you an Administrative Penalty.

Email me at niwasiw@reca.ca, or contact me by phone at 403-685-7938.

Regards,

Nancy Iwasiw
Professional Conduct Review Officer

From: Sly Solutions [mailto:sylvia@slysolutions.ca]
Sent: April-12-16 4:58 PM
To: Nancy Iwasiw
Subject: Re: RECA will issue a penalty to you if you do not respond...

Nancy,

Forgive my brief reply but the fact is that I have explained the nature of my business activities in great detail by both written and verbal methods since January 2013 with Sherry Hillas, Robin Baron, Tricia Hickey, as well as Executive Director Bob Myroniuk.

My business activities help landlords, not hurt them. This is already very clear based on the vexatious complaints coming in to RECA from tenants who are disgruntled and abusing your on-line defamation of my business and my personal character on your website and the information you have posted of me with Better Business Bureau.

I don't believe, and neither does Service Alberta, that RECA's mandate is to be handling tenant and landlord disputes. These tenants should be referred to Residential Tenant Dispute Resolution Services if they have a cause for dispute. There has been no cause for dispute.

The cumulative effects from this on-line defamation and the continuous demand of money from me only cause aggravated pain to me and my family without anyone receiving any gain. It would be much more productive and beneficial to RECA, the public, and myself to allow me to finish out the completion of my existing client contracts.

Unless you are willing to stop demanding money from me for no cause you will only be building a stronger aggravated harassment case for me against RECA. I will follow through appropriately with your civil court action # P1590100760 pre-trial conference call at 1:30 pm on November 24, 2016.

Sylvia Germain

The interrogation continues...

From: Nancy Iwasiw
Sent: Wednesday, April 13, 2016 11:28 AM
To: sylvia@slysolutions.ca
Subject: FW: RECA will issue a penalty to you if you do not respond...

Dear Sylvia,

Thank you for contacting me.

Please allow me to clarify that RECA has not issued any fines as a result of this file (005566) at this time.

My April 5, 2016, email was to advise that if you continued to ignore communications regarding this file we would have no alternative but to issue a Production Order, and failing to comply with that Order can lead to a fine.

Please read my original letter of November 19, 2015. I have attached it again.

This letter was to engage you in dialogue in an attempt to clarify your current activities.

RECA's mandate is to enforce the Real Estate Act. Individuals who trade in real estate in the province of Alberta require a licence. Examples of activities that require a licence include:
- Advertising properties for rent
- Showing properties to prospective tenants
- Negating aspects of a lease on behalf of either the owner or tenant

RECA received information for the property ███████████████████ that indicates you are acting on behalf of an owner in dealing with a tenant. We would agree that tenant disputes are not our jurisdiction. What we our looking at is whether the services you are providing require a licence. When reviewing your website, the services you list on your website, in general, do not require a licence - but some of it is not clear. Your website at slysolutions. ca is advertising several properties. It is unclear what is meant by "property portfolio" – are some of these properties available for rent?

Cooperating with an investigation is a critical factor considered when evaluating the appropriate outcome of an investigation. I would like to offer you another opportunity to answer the questions in the attached letter. With an explanation of what services you provide in general and specifically for ███████████

██████████████ – it may turn out that you don't require a licence for those activities and the file will be closed.

Regards,

Nancy Iwasiw
Professional Conduct Review Officer

2016-04-14   12:55 PM

Nancy,

Let me clarify again that these same questions have been answered numerous times and I will no longer waste my time and sanity entering further dialogue with any RECA officers for vexatious reasons.

Sylvia Germain

Sent: Friday, April 22, 2016 2:47 PM
To: sylvia@slysolutions.ca
Subject: You have until April 29, 2016...

Hello Sylvia,

In my last email to you, dated April 15th, 2016, I gave you an additional opportunity to answer some questions about your current activities. I have attached a copy of that email to this communication.

I would still prefer that we close this file amicably and cooperatively, but I have not heard from you. As I have indicated on more than one occasion, you cannot make this issue go away by ignoring our requests. It does not matter how many times you have spoken with RECA in the past; if RECA gets a new complaint regarding your current activities we are obligated to investigate. *But there was no valid complaint, only a baited catch* I had hoped to help you avoid future complaints by ensuring your business model and marketing leave no room for people to complain that you are trading without a license. *My marketing and website has always been very clear of my distinctive service*

You now have until April 29, 2016 to answer these 6 yes or no questions:
1. Are the properties that appear in the "Property Portfolio" on www.slysolutions.ca advertised for rent?

2. If someone calls you to ask about renting a property, do you put them in contact with the owner?
3. Do only the owners sign lease agreements with tenants?
4. Do all rent and deposit monies go directly from tenants to owners?
5. Does Sly Solutions Ltd. ever hold damage deposits or rent monies in Sly Solutions Ltd. accounts?
6. Do you show properties to prospective tenants?

If you fail to answer the 6 questions (as they appear above) on or before April 29, 2016, RECA will issue you a Production Order as per section 83.2 of the Real Estate Act. You will need to apply to the Court to vary or cancel that Production Order.

Again, I strongly urge you to just answer the 6 questions by email. Understand that your refusal to answer questions will result in a much more serious outcome than was ever intended in this file (005566). *I am not in a court room or a police interrogation and I will not answer "yes or no questions"*

If you have not already spoken to a lawyer about file 005566 and my communications to you (from November 2015 to date), you should do so.

I hope to receive your responses to the six question before April 29, 2016.

Regards,

Nancy Iwasiw
Professional Conduct Review Officer

2016-04-29   7:57 AM

Nancy,

I understand why RECA questioned me in 2013 about my business activities after Carolyn Hackett of Libertas Property Management complained about my existence after I answered her kijiji ad to buy out portfolios. But enough is enough. It's proven Carolyn had been acquiring other portfolios in 2012 and showed a proven deep seated interest in the St. Albert properties I assisted my clients with as a Landlord Agent and poked me many times, in writing, about acquiring my portfolio at the same time RECA began investigating my services. It is also proven in my 2" email correspondence paper file proving RECA's ignorance of my cooperation in explaining my business model numerous times to Sherry Hillas, Tricia Hickey, Bob Myroniuk and most importantly, Carolyn Hackett, that **I did not hold rent money** so I did not have a rent roll to sell over to Carolyn Hackett. I did not hold rent money or deposit money because **I WAS**

NOT ACTING IN THE CAPACITY OF A REAL ESTATE INDUSTRY MEMBER. I AM SIMPLY A LANDLORD AGENT acting in the capacity of a Landlord Agent within the boundaries of the Residential Tenancies Act.

As I have explained numerous times, my website, nor myself, have ever portrayed licensed credentials of any kind or that I buy and sell properties or that I seek to provide services for anything other than privately owned residential units. It has also always been very clear on my website that "MY SERVICE DIFFERS FROM THE COMPETITION" IN THAT THE CLIENT CONTROLS THEIR MONEY. I showcased Moe on my site because whenever my clients wanted actual real estate advice I needed someone I trusted to refer to them and my education in marketing has taught me that establishing identity is important. That is all I did. I have not been running a seedy brokerage just simply offering an honest, valuable and demanded "custom" landlord agent service that your industry members are not providing. The term property manager is just that. A term. Maintenance companies call themselves property management. It is just a common key phrase term that people use to google when they are looking for any kind of assistance with their properties and this ongoing war on semantics is a complete waste of life.

My website is not questionable. The properties showcased on my website do not have active 'For Rent' or 'For Sale' information. **My clients cover the costs for advertising properties on paid rental websites.** You've already indicated previously "When reviewing your website, the services you list on your website, in general, do not require a licence - but some of it is not clear." It is actually very clear. My services are exactly as shown on my website and have not changed and you can leave me and my website alone now that Moe is no longer identified at all on it (even though we were cleared in January 2013 to showcase him after I updated his brokerage information).

The Alberta Residential Tenancies Act specifies that a "Landlord Agent" can be "any person who has been given the authority by another person to undertake certain activities on their behalf". This person can be "a property manager, a leasing agent, caretaker, building manager, or any other person who controls whether someone can rent the place". **The residential property owner can authorize me to perform whatever activities they choose and I have been given the authorization by owners to show property** the same as an **on-site manager** can, a superintendent, a caretaker, or a property manager can so the reason for you even opening file #005566 is vexatious. There is no reference in the Residential Tenancies Act or with Service Alberta that RECA has ANY affiliation what-so-ever with this act, or that an authorized Landlord Agent should be concerned with any form of licensing. **ALL of my services fall within the Landlord and Tenant industry, NOT the real estate industry.**

Section 17 in your Real Estate Act only refers to RECA's authorization to regulate "real estate brokers, mortgage brokers, and real estate appraisers"

and does not include Landlord Agents or even Property Managers (like you've tried to include on your website**).** RECA cannot just adjust the act simply based on their interpretation and you have no right to bully me with the same abuse of power you use with your industry members if I have "**not acted in any capacity as an industry member**".

███████████████████████ of ███████████████ from file #005566 were only disgruntled tenants angry about the owner deciding to sell versus continuing with their ongoing excuses for not signing into an actual lease term. The tenants were given proper 90 day notice to sell and were dealt with professionally even as rude as they were to both myself and the acting realtor who sold the condo. It is proven in writing that this realtor reached out to me a few times for assistance in handling these difficult tenants during their showing process and appreciated my level of knowledge and professionalism. The tenants received their full security deposit back **from the owner** in the appropriate time frame legislated by the Residential Tenancies Act and had no reason for dispute. They were just spoiled entitled rich kids who learned to fight from watching their parents battle through ugly divorce and mad about having to move and found a way to take it out on me with the extortive defamation by RECA of my business on BBB. Your Production Order would only prove that. Again, **working on behalf of a residential property owner for activities authorized by them that are within the Residential Tenancies Act does not require a real estate brokerage license. It also does not warrant cause for these repeated interrogations.**

RECA's harassment has caused great financial, mental, and physical anguish to me and my family and they have wrongfully defamed me with BBB without a court decision proving that I required your unreasonable licensing. Now you have the nerve to tell me that it's possible I may not need a license based on how I answer the same questions I've already answered repeatedly...?!

I take great offense to your disregard of the severity of harassment and extortion that has been dealt to me by all the RECA officers competing for some kind of trophy. The only thing I am guilty of is providing an ethical landlord service and becoming successful enough to evoke malicious action from others who are jealous and lacking that same ethic. Extortion is illegal. My actions are not. **So unless you are willing to close this file and consider my Landlord services as exempt from brokerage licensing and retract the extortive defamation on your website and BBB's website, do not contact me again by any means,** **directly or indirectly.** I will see you in court to claim compensation for ALL my damages as specified in the civil counter claim.

Sylvia Germain

CHAPTER 44
Advance to GO and Collect Much More Than $200...

I was expecting another round with Nancy after my 'tell it like it really is' punch in the gut back to her. After 2 weeks of not hearing from her I was starting to think she actually heard me. She must have been doing her homework by having their legal counsel take a look at the Residential Tenancies Act.

Six weeks had gone by and I still had not received any further swings from her. I wondered if maybe they were busy preparing their production order. How they could demand a production order was beyond me though considering the tenants did not have a valid specified complaint. There was no financial transaction to investigate.

My fears were eased when I received this brief email from her advising me that the complaint file/fight #005566 was CLOSED. OMG!! Really?! My heart began racing with excitement and I had to warn myself not to celebrate until I had finished reading the attached letter:

2016-06-13   10:06 AM

Hi Sylvia,

This email is to advise that file 005566 (complaint from the Bauwens) is now closed.
There are no fines relating to file 005566. Please review the attached letter.

Regards,

Nancy Iwasiw
Professional Conduct Review Officer

Real
Estate
Council
Alberta

June 13, 2016

Private and Confidential

Case: 005566

Sylvia Germain
Sly Solutions Ltd.

Dear Ms. Germain:

Review Outcome: Insufficient Evidence

The Executive Director of the Real Estate Council of Alberta (RECA) has completed a review of your activities to determine whether a licence was required.

Information received during the course of our investigation indicates that you, and Sly Solutions Ltd., are not currently advertising property for sale or rent through slysolutions.ca. Information received suggests that the properties featured on the slysolutions.ca website are images for management portfolio purposes only.

As per the *Real Estate Act* (the Act):

1(1)(s.1) "property management" includes any of the following:

    (i)   leasing or offering to lease real estate or negotiating or approving, or offering to negotiate or approve, a lease or rental of real estate;

    (ii)   holding money received in connection with an activity referred to in subclause (i);

    (iii) advertising, negotiating or carrying out any other activity, directly or indirectly, for the purpose of furthering an activity referred to in subclause (i) or (ii):

RECA Information Bulletin: Holding Oneself Out has been enclosed with this letter. This bulletin describes activities that require authorization.

The authority for a positive real estate experience.

Upon review of information received, there is insufficient evidence your activities require authorization. Accordingly, this review (file 005566) has been closed. Please be advised that any outstanding files or legal action outside of this matter (file 005566) are not affected by the closing of this file. RECA reserves the right to take such further action as the public interest may require.

You are required to cooperate with any such further actions in the future. If you have answered similar questions, or provided explanation(s) of your business model to RECA in the past, it does not prohibit RECA from making any inquiries or requests for information in the future.

Failure to co-operate with an investigation will only prolong and escalate said investigation. Please be aware than non-cooperation is a considered a significant aggravating factor, and that non-cooperation can ultimately result in fines.

RECA hopes that you will recognize any future inquiries and communications from RECA staff as an opportunity for you to inform and assure RECA that your activities are not in breach of the Act, and do not require authorization.

Thank you for you cooperation during this review. If you have any questions, please contact Nancy Iwasiw, Professional Conduct Review Officer, at 403-685-7938 or niwasiw@reca.ca.

Yours truly,

Bob Myroniuk
Executive Director

Enclosed: RECA Information Bulletin: Holding Oneself Out

Let's break this down again. First, it was always made clear that I was not advertising properties for rent or sale on my website. The web page was titled "sample portfolio" not "properties for rent". The six "yes or no" questions she kept trying to trip me up with related to more than just properties being advertised for rent. Hounding me and threatening me with fines and production orders and defaming me for 3 years was not just about me advertising properties for rent on my website so why is this the only reference made to justify the closure of this file? It had to be because they knew I had a case and that I was not doing anything wrong. They did not want to say that though and had to be sure to keep themselves in the driver's seat of their Rolls Royce by attaching more of the same references they always referred to.

Second, I already broke down their "property management" reference in Chapter 20 and in my final letter to Nancy in reference to the Residential Tenancies Act.

As for RECA information bulletins…those are redundant as they represent mere perceptions of the Real Estate Act that RECA chooses to perceive in their favour.

I see another fear mongering attempt by Nancy in her explanation that "Any outstanding files or legal action outside of this matter (file 005566) are not affected by closing this file." So…if there was insufficient evidence in this file/fight #005566 to prove I required a real estate license, what sufficient evidence did they have for file/fight #003228? Absolutely none. They did not even have a specified complainant as they did in file/fight #005566.

I have proven that I cooperated with their initial investigation even though I had a right not to divulge any information until going in front of an Alberta Justice Judge.

What I suffered through in the last 3 years is not about simple name calling in the playground. I have been called names all my life and learned at a young age that those who throw stones at me are either very jealous or hurting inside themselves so I would not let the names hurt me.

I am an adult professional woman who offered a unique ethical rental service that I found a niche market demand for. I used my knowledge and skills to define and market my business model to attract clients who easily understood the fine line and distinction of my services. This industry needs to understand that fine line. My success has unfortunately caused jealousy in others who have chosen to act maliciously in extorting and defaming me to take me down instead of appreciating the differences in our businesses and improving their own self with the same hard work I endured. Just because I did not take the same courses as them does not mean I was getting off easy. If anything, I only worked that much harder to get where I had gotten.

I never did anything wrong yet that jealousy from others had destroyed my business, my mental status, my physical ability, and my faith. I lost much more than just a little self-confidence from name calling by mean girls.

I lost past, present and future income that I cannot replace. I lost precious happy times with my teenage daughter due to depression from stress and fear. I lost relationships because I was unable to focus on anything other than the constant negative pressure upon me. I lost my passion for work and life. My family also suffered in worry for me.

I had to embark on a very deep spiritual journey to start coming out of this black rabbit hole I was railroaded into. I expect I may never come all the way out until I find justice. I do not wish badly on the women, and men, who were so relentless in destroying me. I do wish that if, and when, they read this that they become sympathetic of what I endured and realize themselves that there is more power to be gained by following their mandate in serving the public versus abusing their power to serve themselves. I wish to instill emotion in people to spark the notion to think of win-win solutions rather than win-lose power struggles.

I do not know what the result will be of the November 24, 2016 telephone conference but if there is justice in this realm of earth I trust it will appear for me and that I will be allowed a fair trial. I hope that I will also be compensated fairly not only for my losses but for the immeasurable time that has been stolen from my life, and my daughter's life, in addressing this situation with countless letters and thoughts and research and anxiety.

It is difficult to determine how much income I could have earned in the last 3 years if I had not been defamed and if there had not been a choke hold on me to advertise. I might have even been able to franchise this landlord agent business model that I had come so close towards achieving. My lost income is however measurable based on my previous two years' average annual income. By the time the gavel falls on this case the loss will be significant enough to be heard by the highest court.

I have been robbed of the rights and freedoms granted by our Canadian Charter of Rights and Freedoms. I have truly suffered defamation of both my business and personal character. My immediate and long term financial security has been significantly compromised as well as my psychological integrity. The psychological integrity of my daughter has been compromised. My relationships with family, friends, and clients, have been compromised. The public is being denied a protective transparent service that they have a right to seek. I believe RECA's motives for defaming me is also transparent. What do *you* think…?

Afterward

Sun Life Update

Sun Life has not denied me the coverages they threatened to revoke however I never did receive the letter of retraction. I only received a verbal apology on my answering machine. I still have to fight with Sun Life for almost every claim I make no matter how thorough I am in providing information.

For example, my daughter was referred for counselling with a certified, and registered, psychologist for anxiety. It was obvious my suffering caused her suffering. I submitted my claim of $525, which my plan booklet says is covered, and they have denied me reimbursement 3 times already. The first was denied because I did not include a doctor's written prescription for the counselling. I had to go to my doctor and ask for a written prescription that I stapled to that claim statement with a handwritten note on the statement to refer to the doctor's prescription attached.

I was denied a second time and went through 30 minutes of hassle to get the department I had requested in my first round of "press this for…". I was told they had not received the doctor's prescription, only the previous statement of claim with my handwritten note. I'm so sure. Somebody had to tear that staple out for it to go missing…?!

I demand an email or fax number to forward the doctor's prescription and was provided a fax number to which I faxed it to. The following week it was denied again with the note "The prescription provided does not indicate doctor's credential. Please resubmit with a prescription from a medical doctor."

Ok, this is the shit that makes me understand why people go bat shit crazy and walk into official offices and fire rounds. The very top of the full 8" x 11" computerized prescription indicated the name of the medical clinic and my doctor's name in big bolded capital letters. It included the address, phone, number, fax number, Rx pharmacy symbol and detailed directions referring my daughter to the name of the specified psychologist for counselling purposes. It included the doctor's signature and assisting practitioner's signature PLUS the stamp with the medical clinic information and pharmacist notes area. It was the same friggin' prescription format I have been providing Sun Life for 3 years already.

It's hard to handle such incompetency at the same time that I'm being stuffed down a black rabbit hole for competency issues.

I don't even bother with getting massages I really need. The two times I scheduled with a therapist who offered direct billing for Sun Life there were complications forcing me to pay up front and make a manual paper claim. Whatever.

P.S. I am now 20 lbs heavier than I was at the beginning of 2013.

BBB Update

As of August 2016 the slanderous RECA blurb advising the world of "Government Action" against me has been removed. My rating is still an "F" however due to: "Failure to have a required competency license". I am very competent. This still defames both me and my business.

BBB Business Review

THIS BUSINESS IS NOT BBB ACCREDITED.

Sly Solutions Ltd

Phone: (780) 458-5008
View Additional Phone Numbers
Address on File, St. Albert, AB T8N 6H8
http://www.slysolutions.ca

On a scale of A+ to F
Reason for Rating
BBB Ratings System Overview

BBB Business Reviews may not be reproduced for sales or promotional purposes.

BBB Accreditation

This business is not BBB accredited.

Businesses are under no obligation to seek BBB accreditation, and some businesses are not accredited because they have not sought BBB accreditation.

To be accredited by BBB, a business must apply for accreditation and BBB must determine that the business meets BBB accreditation standards, which include a commitment to make a good faith effort to resolve any consumer complaints. BBB Accredited Businesses must pay a fee for accreditation review/monitoring and for support of BBB services to the public.

Reason for Rating

BBB rating is based on 13 factors. Get the details about the factors considered.

Factors that *lowered* the rating for Sly Solutions Ltd include:

Failure to have a required competency license

Factors that *raised* the rating for Sly Solutions Ltd include:

Length of time business has been operating
No complaints filed with BBB

Customer Complaints Summary

http://www.bbb.org/edmonton/business-reviews/real-estate-rental-service/sly-solutions-ltd-in-st-albert-ab-160872/

241

0 complaints closed with BBB in last 3 years | 0 closed in last 12 months

Complaint Type	Total Closed Complaints
Advertising/Sales Issues	0
Billing/Collection Issues	0
Delivery Issues	0
Guarantee/Warranty Issues	0
Problems with Product/Service	0
Total Closed Complaints	0

Definitions | BBB Complaint Process | File a Complaint against Sly Solutions Ltd

Customer Reviews Summary   Read customer reviews

0 Customer Reviews on Sly Solutions Ltd

Customer Experience	Total Customer Reviews
Positive Experience	0
Neutral Experience	0
Negative Experience	0
Total Customer Reviews	0

Read Customer Reviews | Submit a Customer Review | See Trends in Customer Reviews on Sly Solutions Ltd

Government Actions

BBB knows of no government actions involving the marketplace conduct of Sly Solutions Ltd.

What government actions does BBB report on?

Advertising Review

BBB has nothing to report concerning Sly Solutions Ltd's advertising at this time.

What is BBB Advertising Review?

Additional Information

BBB file opened: May 26, 2011
Business started: 01/01/2010
Business started locally: 01/01/2010
Business incorporated 02/23/2009 in

Business Management

http://www.bbb.org/edmonton/business-reviews/real-estate-rental-service/sly-solutions-ltd-in-st-albert-ab-160872/

Pre-Trial Hearing Update

The run around involved with the justice system regarding this case has become lengthy and harrowing enough to warrant a second book. It has uncovered even more layers of corruption.

I will stand strong with conviction in standing up against corporate tyranny because I have no better choice. I have nothing left to lose and everything to gain from rallying against this Real Estate Council of Alberta and seeking vindication and restitution.

My annual revenue for Sly Solutions Ltd has dropped from $100,000 to less than $50,000. I still remain unemployable for permanent positions regardless of how many resumes I submit or how many headhunters I have seeking opportunities for me.

The pre-trial telephone conference in November 2016 did result in a court date being scheduled for October 18, 2017 in Calgary, AB but I had to incur further legal costs to apply to have that court hearing transferred to Edmonton, where it should rightfully be. On May 5, 2017, the Calgary court finally approved my request to transfer this hearing to Edmonton where it lawfully should be. I will still need to convince an Edmonton small claims judge of the justification in transferring this case to Court of Queen's Bench. My claim for damages has been revised to $515,000, or better. It is September 2017, it has already cost me over $20,000 in legal fees, and I am still waiting for that Edmonton court date. Not surprisingly, the court has lost my file.

To be continued…

Acknowledgements

Many thought I was wasting my time and money trying to fight a whole pride of lions by myself so I want to give special thanks to the family and friends who actually have supported my quest for vindication. I don't know how my mother had the strength to continue taking every one of my pitiful phone calls of despair.

I want to thank Moe for staying on board in business, and friendship, with me for as long as he did. He could have jumped ship at the first poke by RECA but he believed in my transparent business model and supported my decision to stand strong for my clients. When I finally do get vindication and a settlement for my damages I will reimburse him the $1500 fine that he paid to RECA 3 years after he had already been given the green light to continue working with me.

Thank you to my doctor and psychologist for their validation of the stress I was experiencing and helping me to find my inner strength and power again.

Thank you to my publishing company, who expressed genuine empathy for my story and related with my position as an "industry disruptor".

I did express gratitude to many others in relevant chapters so, please read the book to find your special mention ;)

Resources the Author Recommends

Guide to Canadian Charter of Rights and Freedoms
https://www.canada.ca/en/canadian-heritage/services/
how-rights-protected/guide-canadian-charter-rights-freedoms.html

Alberta Bullying Recovery, Resources, Research Centre Inc.
www.abrc.ca

Competition Bureau of Canada
https://www.canada.ca/en/competition-bureau/news/2018/01/growing_
the_new_economytheintegralrelationshipbetweencompetition.html

Anderson Career Training Institute www.acti.org

Alberta Residential Landlord Association (formerly Edmonton
Apartment Association) www.albertalandlord.org

Edmonton Landlord and Tenant Advisory Board - www.edmonton.ca/
programs_services/housing/landlord-and-tenant-advisory-board.aspx

Residential Tenancy Dispute Resolution Service (RTDRS)
http://servicealberta.ca/landlord-tenant-disputes.cfm

Alberta Ombudsman www.ombudsman.ab.ca

You are welcome to join me, and welcome others to join us, in
sharing your bullying/defamation stories or your support at:
www.slysolutions.ca/contactme

18320591R00140

Made in the USA
San Bernardino, CA
21 December 2018